"I love how Jenny walks us through creative prompts th[...] *Courageous Creative* is a near-perfect spark for out-of-the [...] one looking for creative moments in dormant areas of e[...] ing outside the lines to capturing photos with your point of view, it helps a creative journey truly flourish. Plus, it's just old-fashioned fun!"

—**Candace Payne**
viral sensation and author of *Laugh It Up, Defiant Joy,* and *Simple Joys*

"*Courageous Creative* provides a biblical view of your creativity and empowers you with the truth that you *are* creative! You were made to make stuff that brings glory to your Creator. Jenny helps you uncover your creativity and live it out amid life's chaos. This book spoke deeply to me and uncovered what I didn't know was hidden in the corners of my heart. Now I'm pursuing painting after years of thinking I was no good at it, and I'm using my God-given creative gifts in my business without fear or timidity. This book is such a gift to the world!"

—**Allie Casazza**
host of *The Purpose Show* podcast

"I absolutely love this book! As an artsy storyteller, Jenny helps you unearth areas you've never explored in a fun way. You'll look forward to trying each new activity and exploring more of the creative side of God along the way."

—**Rebecca Bender**
author, speaker, and advocate

"Everyone can be creative. Every. Single. Person. Most of us just need a nudge in the right direction—and *Courageous Creative* is that nudge. It's a devotional, inspirational guide, instruction manual, and activity book all rolled into one fun package. If you want to stretch and develop your creative muscles, this is the tool for you."

—**Jonathan Malm**
author of *The Hidden Option* and *Created for More*

"It's time to let go of the things that limit our ability to dream with God and to listen as the Holy Spirit empowers us to create and bring glory to Christ. *Courageous Creative* speaks the truth into your creative process—and provides loads of fun. Jenny's book will awaken your childlike wonder and challenge you to dream again!"

—**Jamie Ivey**
host of the *Happy Hour* podcast and author of *If You Only Knew*

"Freedom often finds us through a song lyric or words spoken from a stage or written in a book. Our creativity makes space for life-changing moments to happen in people. That's why this book is so important. Jenny reveals the deeper things that kill our creativity, and she empowers us to become more creative along the way. *Courageous Creative* is a must-have book to spark your creative soul."

—Carlos Whittaker
speaker and author of *Moment Maker* and *Kill the Spider*

"This book will make you laugh out loud and challenge you to be more creative than you have before. Jenny is the new best friend you've been searching for. She will remind you what it was like to be creative before your brain got in the way."

—Katie Allred
cofounder of ChurchCommunications.com and professor at the University of Mobile

"With a funny, inspiring, and 'I feel like she's talking to me' kind of narrative, *Courageous Creative* is an interactive journey that breathes new life into our creative bones. Jenny's prompts, mixed with truth from the Word of God and deep revelations uncovered by one who has spent time in His presence, left me feeling free to be who I was designed to be. Jenny inspires and encourages you to walk in your true identity and to let your creativity blossom. *Courageous Creative* helped me to return to a childlike place of creating by remembering the joy that comes with imagining and playing with God. I know you will love this tool as much as I have!

—Michelle Lutz
worship leader, songwriter, and creative pastor

"I picked up *Courageous Creative* because I'm a fan of Jenny Randle. I knew her book would be gorgeously crafted, because I follow her work. I also knew this would be a fun, entertaining, and inspiring journey. What I wasn't prepared for is how empowering the challenges in *Courageous Creative* would be. When I think of creatives, I think of artists, graphic designers, performers... people with talents I do not have. Yet this book is a beautiful reminder that God has called and equipped all of us to create. Jenny, well done."

—Shauna Shanks
speaker and author of *A Fierce Love*

COURAGEOUS
CREATIVE

Jenny Randle

HARVEST HOUSE PUBLISHERS

EUGENE, OREGON

Coloring pages designed by Danielle Rogers

Interior design by Janelle Coury

Cover design by Connie Gabbert Design + Illustration

Cover photos © simonidadjordjevic / iStockphoto; Illustrations by Connie Gabbert

Published in association with the Steve Laube Agency, LLC, 24 W. Camelback Rd. A-635, Phoenix, Arizona 85013.

Courageous Creative

Copyright © 2018 by Jenny Randle
Published by Harvest House Publishers
Eugene, Oregon 97408
www.harvesthousepublishers.com

ISBN 978-0-7369-7504-9 (pbk.)

Printed in the United States of America

18 19 20 21 22 23 24 25 26 / VP-JC / 10 9 8 7 6 5 4 3 2 1

To every wounded creative or procrastinating dreamer

Rediscover the freedom to create again.
The world needs you to shine.

Contents

After you complete each day's challenge, check it off here.

ACT 3: UNLEASH CREATIVITY

A Note from Jenny

Have you had moments that marked your timeline in life? You can point back to them and say, "That's when…" I call those "magical Jesus moments."

That's when I knew I was supposed to be a musician.

That's when God became real to me.

That's when I met my spouse.

They are moments when time slows, and it's as if heaven aligns the tiniest details to create something special. These moments shape your character, inspire you to dream, and draw you closer to the Creator of all things.

Perhaps you had a magical Jesus moment the first time you acted on a stage or scored the winning goal. Maybe it happened when you built a pinewood derby car or danced in a way that made you feel alive. Mine came on a snowy day in third grade when my teacher watched my first "film." That was the moment I fell in love with the power of storytelling.

Our childhood is filled with imagination and exploration that can lead us down a path of creative discovery and wonderment. But sometimes these defining moments become distant memories, buried beneath the everyday hustle of life. Responsibilities pile up, and before we know it, we hear ourselves saying, "I'm not creative," or "I don't have time for that."

My creativity nearly got beaten down by a battle with depression and insecurity. Maybe you have a similar story. There were a lot of magical Jesus moments that led to my professional career as a creative ninja. Overcoming that battle with depression was one of them. (And all the praise hands go to Jesus!)

My prayer for you is that you will know you're valuable. And that you will trust God to help you overcome any obstacle that stands in your way of creating courageously.

What if Holy Spirit (who is so personal, I drop the "the" before His name) empowered you to dream with God and create again? What if the magical Jesus moments from your own childhood awakened a creative adventure in your life today?

The talents and gifts you may have buried are invaluable assets needed in the world. Cultivating those creative gifts could launch you into your destiny.

So, fellow creative ninja, join me in this faith journey toward creativity. Invite your bro or sista from another mister and commit to developing your creativity together over the next 31 days. The world is waiting to be blessed on the other end of your investment.

I believe that God wants to use you to make an impact on our culture and powerfully influence it for Christ. Cue the music and go high-five another human. Let's do this thing!

Happy creating—you're designed for it!

WE CREATE TO COMMUNICATE
A MESSAGE THAT IS WEIGHING
ON OUR HEARTS OR STIRRING
IN OUR SOULS.

What Is *Courageous Creative?*

It's an interactive journey that will strengthen your creativity and your faith. You'll experience fresh creative and spiritual freedom, discover your God-given identity, and cultivate your creativity.

Supplies You'll Need

camera, video camera, or smartphone

Bible

pen or pencil

computer or smartphone

colored pencils

awesomeness

a willingness to commit

a spirit to do hard things

Rules to Follow

1.

There are no rules...as long as you promise not to use this book for firewood.

2.

This book includes a short message and at least one creative challenge each day. The challenges consist of art, performance, digital story, creative process, photography, freestyle, and written exercises. When you complete a challenge, check it off on the contents page.

3.

Suggested time for the daily creative challenges is seven to ten minutes. Why seven to ten? "Research has shown that just 7 to 10 minutes a day of healthy thinking results in positive improvements in your happiness, peace, health and intelligence."[1]

4.

We suggest reading act 1, The Foundation, in order. Then, if you're feeling spontaneous, feel free to jump between acts 2 and 3 ("Creativity Killers" and "Unleash Your Creativity") as needed.

5.

This is an interactive experience, so we've provided reflective questions, coloring pages (scattered throughout the book), and empty space where you can get creative. Get messy in these pages. Doodle, sketch, highlight, spill your coffee on them...be free.

6.

Have fun. Express yourself in new ways!

7.

Use #courageouscreative so we can get social and cheer you on in your journey.

8.

Think outside the box...remember, there are no rules.

Commitment Contract

Remember when *Who Wants to Be a Millionaire?* was cool and the contestant got to phone a friend? Now is your time! There's power in community and asking a friend for help. Phone a trusted friend and ask him or her to hold you accountable to finish this book. Better yet, buy the person a copy and do it together!

I, _____, commit to cultivating my creativity for 31 days. I'm willing to get uncomfortable so I can stretch and grow. I'm believing Jesus will work in and through me throughout this process.

My accountability partner is _____.

This person committed to encourage me to do hard things.

_____   _____
your creative ninja signature   *date*

_____   _____
accountability partner signature   *date*

ACT 1

THE FOUNDATION

CREATIVITY IS THE ACT
OF MAKING *STUFF*.

Creative Assessment

*Every child is an artist. The problem is
staying an artist when you grow up.*

PABLO PICASSO

We locked the bathroom door behind us and sat on the cold tile floor. Even as a little kid, I knew the acoustics of that place were nothing short of a miracle.

"Action!" my older sister directed as she pressed the play and record buttons simultaneously on the tape deck.

I took the mic, and we began recording our "radio show." We talked about our Barbies and the latest additions to our sticker collections. Important, hard-hitting news, people. My favorite segment involved making animal noises and inviting people to guess what they were. I was horrible at it, which made it even more fun!

Fast-forward 20 years. Three friends and I are sitting in a booth at Bob's Big Boy in North Hollywood.

"Shhhhwaaaaammmmpppp!"

"Wiishhhhhhhhhhh bangggg!"

There we were, four (semi)professional adults, making noises with our mouths. As we waited for our burgers, we decided to test our creativity by playing the sound effects game. It's a slightly advanced version of the animal game I played as a child.

Turns out, I'm still horrible at it...but A for effort, right?

Quick—utilizing only your mouth, make the sound of a door opening and then slamming shut.

Did you do it?

☐ Yes, I'm awesome.   ☐ No, I'm lame.

This book is a spontaneous expression of creativity, so be on your toes, creative ninja. You'll walk away with an A for effort—all you have to do is try.

Throughout this book, you'll find fun activities designed for creatives who want to be intentional about breaking out of the box. Take yourself to the next level in your storytelling craft and learn to embrace your childlike wonder as you communicate the message of your heart.

WHAT IS CREATIVITY?

In its simplest form, creativity is the act of making *stuff*. Sometimes our creativity is expressed through...

- capturing a photo that connects a person's heart to the mission field
- making up jokes that make people smile
- designing a set that captivates the imagination
- developing a new recipe that awakens the taste buds
- leading people into worship in a way that stirs people's hearts to reflect on God
- writing thought-provoking words in a social media post
- communicating in a new way that deepens relationship

Welcome to the opening act of this book. This first act, The Foundation, establishes the main characters and the environment we live in. As you take the following creative assessment, you'll understand where you've been and where you currently stand creatively.

DAY 1
Creative Challenge

CREATIVE PROCESS
ASSESSMENT

Think back to some of your most creative childhood experiences. Maybe you were a set designer who built blanket forts for your Army action figures. Did you construct buildings out of blocks or dance uninhibited in the movie theater during *The Little Mermaid*?

As a child, how did you use your imagination? List the ways you were creative.

1.   4.

2.   5.

3.   6.

7.   9.

8.   10.

What creative activities do you gravitate toward now? Are you a problem solver, gardener, or graphic designer? Think in various contexts, including your hobbies, jobs, parenting, or relationships. Don't limit your answers.

1.   6.

2.   7.

3.   8.

4.   9.

5.   10.

Don't worry if you weren't able to fill in the blanks. We'll figure it out together as we walk out this process. Check out pages 20–21 for some inspiration.

Compare your two creativity lists.
Is your current creative culture as innovative as your preschool mind?

☐ NO   ☐ YES

You're not alone. All of us have felt this way at some point. Throughout this book, you'll find creative challenges, Scriptures, and stories to help you find creative freedom again.

You are in a great position! You can apply these lessons and challenges to encourage your coworkers, family members, or peers to dive deeper into their creativity as you dive deeper into your own.

Globally, 75 percent of adults think they're not living up to their creative potential.[1] It's time to grant ourselves permission to dream with God and create again. After all...

WE ARE DESIGNED FOR IT!

50 WAYS TO BE

Creativity can be displayed in many different ways. Some items on this list aren't often labeled as "creative." Preaching the Gospel or public speaking? That's creative because you're communicating in a strategic way to hold an audience's attention while drawing them into your content. Organizing your space entails problem solving (*Where's all this junk going?*) and can create room for ideas to flow. Working out can create space for your mind to wander and can jump-start the creative process. Henry David Thoreau wrote, "The moment my legs begin to move, my thoughts begin to flow."[2] This infographic is filled with ideas that will build your creative muscles. Look through it and use that smart mind of yours to think about how each activity is creative.

PERFORMANCE

- Learn a new instrument
- Make up silly songs
- Join a band
- Freestyle rap (come on, somebody!)
- Hold a dance party
- Make up new characters and act them out
- Act out your favorite TV show scene

WRITING

- Start a diary and spill your guts
- Write a movie script
- Write a story
- Blog about your interests
- Write a poem and recite it publicly

MEDIA OR PRODUCTION

- Record sound effects using odd objects
- Make a video that tells a story
- Make something out of a cardboard box
- Capture photos of things you love
- Tell a story using graphic design

COMMUNICATION

- Be strategic in your storytelling and give a speech
- Preach the Gospel
- Stand up for a cause you are passionate about
- Meet someone new and introduce yourself
- Ask questions
- Interview someone you look up to

CREATIVE

DESIGN

- Decorate your favorite space
- Build a fort
- Design clothes and costumes for characters

ART AND CRAFTING

- Paint your favorite place to go
- Draw a portrait of yourself
- Create something from clay
- Write using calligraphy
- Do a craft
- Take a drawing lesson on the internet
- Make a collage
- Start a scrapbook
- Knit or sew something

CREATIVE PROCESS AND DEVELOPMENT

- Organize your space
- Read books that stir your imagination
- Make a list for a project you are working on
- Set up a stand and sell something you made
- Research a topic that interests you
- Invent something from scratch
- Conduct a science experiment
- Take something apart and put it back together
- Brainstorm ways to solve a problem
- Do something that relates to STEM (science, technology, engineering and math)

OTHER

- Learn a new sport
- Ready, set, go! Run, walk, or work out
- Grab ingredients and cook
- Bake something yummy
- Plant a garden

Congratulations!

You just finished day 1 of this creativity journey. Reminder: Don't forget to check it off on the contents page. Go celebrate by having a dance party.

GOD IS THE ULTIMATE CREATOR.

Awe-Inspiring Creator

action verbs: *describe activities*

*In the beginning God **created** the heavens and the earth. Now the earth was formless and empty, darkness was over the surface of the deep, and the Spirit of God was **hovering** over the waters. And God **said**, "Let there be light," and there was light. God **saw** that the light was good, and he **separated** the light from the darkness.*

GENESIS 1:1-4

The first words in the Bible show God actively making something new.

These words don't say He loves us, although He does. Or He'll die for us, which He did. The Bible starts by setting the foundation of God as Creator. He created the heavens and the earth.

From Genesis to Revelation, beginning to end, God is in the business of making something out of nothing.[1] He's in a constant state of revealing ideas and bringing things into existence. **"Creator" is God's first character trait communicated in the Bible.** It's a powerful, creative expression of who He is and what He does.

IN SIMPLE TERMS... GOD MAKES *STUFF*.

Almost every summer of elementary school, I went away to sleepover camp. The summer days consisted of swimming, arts and crafts, and team-building exercises. (I'm basically the queen of the trust fall.) One night, my fellow campers and I ditched our cozy cabin and hiked into the mountains. Fifty young kids covered in mosquito repellent and a few brave counselors marched deep into the woods searching for something bigger than ourselves...and it wasn't a bear.

> **FUN FACT**
> In the Old Testament, "created" (Hebrew: *bārā'*) consistently refers to a new activity.[2]

After what seemed like hours of hiking and being on high alert for animal attacks, we reached an open clearing. The day faded as we snuggled into the warmth of our sleeping bags. I clung to my flashlight as it produced a comforting light in a moment when I felt so small underneath the vast darkness of the night sky.

In the middle of stories, boys passing gas, and girls giggling, a flash shot across the sky...and another, and another. Shooting stars were suddenly filling the sky with a dance all their own. It's the reason we hiked to the open clearing—to catch a glimpse of the night sky performing.

It was breathtaking.

Laying there still, under the darkness of the sky, I believed in the creativity of God.

Have you experienced a moment that made you believe in an awe-inspiring God?

Do you believe when you see fireflies glowing in rhythmic motion or snow glistening in a child's outstretched hands...or have you missed it? Sometimes *life happens*, and even when I'm standing under the stars, I miss their twinkle. Or I'll race from place to place but miss out on actually seeing the faces of others.

Can you relate? When was the last time you sat in solitude and expressed gratitude for all God has created?

Genesis 1 describes the creation of the world. Grab your Bible and check it out—you'll start hugging those trees in no time.

Creation reflects the glory of God. So whether you are appreciating the sunrise that symbolizes a new day, learning about the creation of the stars, or standing in awe at the wonders of the waves, make time to notice God's handiwork.[3] **When we live in thankful intention, we'll see another dimension of our awe-inspiring Creator.**

WRITING
CREATIVE NATURE

Take action and get moving. Go for a hike or just stand under the stars for inspiration. **Using action verbs, write out short descriptions of the things God has created around you.** Meditate on Genesis 1 if you need inspiration, and don't forget to ask Holy Spirit to inspire this process. Give thanks to Him for taking action and filling the once-empty canvas!

Examples: "God beautifully *designed* the peacock," "He *colored* the ocean the perfect tint of teal…"

DAY 2
Creative Challenge

It was our Creator who gave us the ability to create and dream with the same passion and love He used to paint the stars in the sky.

Jeremy Adams, Hollywood screenwriter and producer

YOU CAN'T UNDERSTAND
CREATIVITY FROM A BIBLICAL
PERSPECTIVE WITHOUT FIRST
UNDERSTANDING GOD'S
RELATIONAL NATURE.

Relationship

God, who said, "Let light shine out of darkness," made his light shine in our hearts to give us the light of the knowledge of God's glory displayed in the face of Christ.

2 CORINTHIANS 4:6

My husband, Matt, taught me to surf once. He connects with God in nature and wanted me to experience his "paradise."

Matt's a teach-by-doing sort of guy, so he pushed me out into the intimidating waves and yelled for me to paddle. Swinging my arms in a panicked poetic motion, I moved with the board as if I were one with the ocean. Just as I started thinking I was the coolest chick in town, a massive wave plunged my ego and body into the depths of the ocean. Underwater, I was spinning in a washing-machine vortex. Up was down and down was up. Disoriented, I became desperate. I was sinking like Katy Perry's left shark in the Super Bowl, surrounded by nothing but the darkness of the sea. I was lost, holding my breath, waiting for someone to pull me up from the chaos.

Then, a glimmer of hope. Shining in the darkness, there was a tiny ray of light—just enough to guide me out of the spin cycle and into the arms of safety.

My (almost) surfing tragedy is an illustration of how God wants to be in relationship with us and bring us out of the chaos in our own lives. The Ultimate Creator is constantly shining light into dark areas and making things new as Holy Spirit moves. Remember yesterday how we considered the way God created the heavens and the earth? **Isn't it amazing how the earth being formed and brought out of darkness can be a direct parallel to our salvation experience?**

In what way has God led you out of darkness?

IF YOU ARE CURRENTLY FEELING LIKE YOU'RE DROWNING, I CHALLENGE YOU TO ASK GOD TO SHOW YOU HIS LIGHT.

When I was a senior in high school, I found Jesus at a church play. My friend and I sat in the back, our blond ponytails a stark contrast to the sea of church hats. I was navigating the end of my teenage years with boy drama that left me feeling hurt, confused, and worthless. I thought being invited to a play at a small-town Protestant church would be a good distraction.

The church had two projector screens and uplighting that accented the stage design. That level of production in a church was new to me. Captivated, I leaned in as the play began with actor-Jesus walking down the aisle bearing the weight of the cross. A series of skits unfolded. Bright lights flashed as prerecorded angelic voices sang from the speakers.

I was hooked.

The creativity of the experience and the message of the gospel pulled on my heartstrings. There I was in all my teenage angst, contemplating the most spiritually challenging question I'd ever faced.

DID I WANT A RELATIONSHIP WITH JESUS?

In that moment, I didn't feel afraid of the unknown. Instead, I felt known by a loving God.

Holy Spirit opened my eyes to see that I was a sinner in need of a Savior and that He designed me to be in relationship with Him.[1] His love and grace was greater than my sin, guilt, or shame. I was forgiven. I was new.[2] Becoming a Christian that day was the most radical and best moment I've ever had. **God spoke life into my situation, and my once-chaotic world became calmer.**

Are you in the midst of your own personal chaos? Do you feel like you're drowning under the untamed waves? In the Gospels, the disciples woke Jesus in the middle of a storm. They asked, "Don't you care if we drown?"

With a creative comeback, Jesus responded by getting up and commanding the storm to be calm.[3]

Whatever stage of faith you're in, whether you're feeling secure in your boat or holding your breath under the waves, meet God there. Ask Him if He cares if you drown. Like a child reaching for a father, you can reach to God, and He will wrap you in an embracing love and calm the storms of life.

Are you wondering why knowing Jesus is in a book about creativity? It's because you can't understand creativity from a biblical perspective without first understanding God's relational nature. Pages 30–31 illustrate the most beautiful love story ever encountered. It's a redemptive story that shows we are created for companionship with the Creator of the universe.

SIMPLE PRAYER

Thank You, Jesus, for giving us new life. We love You! Amen.

Review these tips to prepare for the upcoming photo challenge.

1. Create depth by having something in the foreground, middle ground and background. Having something so close in the foreground it seems like you can touch it is especially effective. It makes you feel like you're right there.

2. Use something in the environment to create a visual frame around your subject. It could be a literal frame, like a window frame, or something in the foreground or background of the image.

PHOTOGRAPHY
COMPOSITION

Take a photo representing this verse: "If anyone is in Christ, the new creation has come: The old has gone, the new is here!" (2 Corinthians 5:17).

Work on your composition and frame it in a unique and compelling way.

Using your smartphone? Hold it horizontally to utilize a larger canvas.

THE GOOD NEWS

GOD CREATED YOU IN HIS OWN IMAGE and made you unique.

Have you ever made a selfish choice or done something deliberately wrong?

Sometimes you can get in the way of knowing God.

THE BIBLE CALLS THIS "SIN."

Sin changes us and makes it difficult for us to receive God's love.

The result of sin is that we cannot approach God. (But keep reading—it gets better.)

God wants to be in relationship with us, so He sent Jesus.

Jesus Christ LIVED a perfect life on earth,

TOOK OUR SINS upon Himself,

DIED on the cross, conquering sin's hold on us,

and ROSE again.

Because Jesus died for us, we can be a part of God's family for eternity.

This is the best gift ever.

FROM THE BIBLE

"If you openly declare that Jesus is Lord and believe in your heart that God raised Him from the dead, you will be saved" (Romans 10:9 NLT).

The moment we ask for forgiveness from our sins (repent),

by God's grace and love,

WE ARE FORGIVEN.

When you surrender your life to Christ, God sends His Holy Spirit to guide you.

Holy Spirit brings love, joy, peace, patience, kindness, goodness, faithfulness, gentleness, and self-control.

You will be radically transformed from the inside out!

If you would like to receive Jesus Christ as your Savior,

you can pray a simple prayer to God

ACKNOWLEDGING YOUR FAILURES,

accepting His forgiveness,

PUTTING YOUR FAITH IN CHRIST,

and pursuing a relationship with this passionately loving God.

GOD BIRTHED THE WORLD INTO
EXISTENCE AND SPOKE LIFE INTO
THE LIFELESS. FROM THE DUST
OF THE GROUND, A BREATH OF
LIFE CREATED A LIVING BEING.

Created to Create

The LORD God formed the man from the dust of the ground. He breathed the breath of life into the man's nostrils, and the man became a living person.

GENESIS 2:7 NLT

Have you ever wondered, *Where did I come from?* Before your eyes glaze over and you start to dream of pizza or the newest episode of *This Is Us*, I need you to focus. This will help to build the foundation of your creativity. God's fingerprint is woven throughout our anatomy! Our body is an intricately designed, wonderfully made, creative miracle.[1]

God created us. Got it? Let's take it a step further...

Researcher Ginger Allen writes, "God breathed into man the breath of life. The terms *Spirit* and *breath*, in reference to God's, are often used interchangeably. God's breath is His Spirit. God exhaled His breath into the body that He had formed, giving man not only an earthly origin but a divine one."[2]

"God created human beings in his own image. In the image of God he created them; male and female he created them" (Genesis 1:27 NLT). Which means **our human spirit reflects God's divine attributes.** Since He is the Ultimate Creator and we reflect Him, that means...you guessed it, we are *all* born creative! So the next time you hear somebody say, "I'm not creative," ninja chop him or her with some Genesis 1:27.

YOU ARE MADE IN THE IMAGE OF THE ULTIMATE
CREATOR. CREATIVITY IS IN YOUR DNA.

It's biblical and scientific. Dr. George Land conducted a research study to test the creativity of children as they aged. The results were amazing and eye-opening.[3]

IMAGINATION AND CREATIVITY
DECREASE WITH AGE

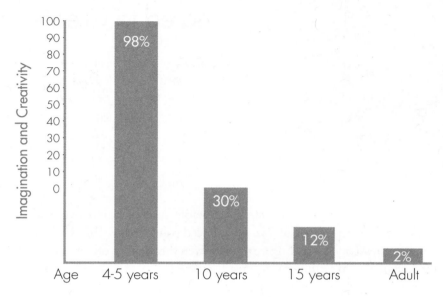

DR. GEORGE LAND'S CREATIVITY STUDY

Five-year-olds tested at 98 percent and are considered creative geniuses! By age 31, the level of creativity decreased to 2 percent. As you can see, creativity drastically decreases as age increases.

Aren't you glad you are reading this interactive devotional?

Sometimes we can lose our creative nature because of sin, shame, rules, or pain. We'll explore those further in act 2, Creativity Killers, and we'll retrain our creative minds.

As adults, let's return to that childlike wonder of play and get out of our own way.

Be silly.

Be free.

Be who God created you to be.

"What we have concluded is that non-creative behavior is learned."

George Land

SIMPLE PRAYER

God, help us to start living out Your creative nature. Amen!

ANNA TAUBE
actor, singer, and music teacher

SIX TIPS TO HELP YOU MASTER THE MONOLOGUE

1. Use good body language by standing tall with shoulders back, both feet planted on the ground and head held high.

2. Keep your hands by your side, and refrain from pulling at your clothes.

3. Project your voice toward the back of the room.

4. Be mindful of how quickly you're speaking.

5. Articulate your words so nothing is lost.

6. Make time to pause and be still. The moments of silence and stillness are actually where people reflect the most on their own experiences. That's how you can tell an experienced actor from an amateur.

DAY 4
Creative Challenge

PERFORMANCE
THE MONOLOGUE

Using your smartphone, record yourself giving a short monologue. Find your own or read a section from the Creative Manifesto on the next page. Bonus points if you post it on social media using **#courageouscreative**.

THE CREATIVE MANIFESTO

My God is creative.

He birthed the world into existence and spoke life into the lifeless.
From the dust of the ground, a breath of life created a living being.
In the image of God, I am made.

WHOLE. UNIQUE. **PURPOSED**.

Creativity is in my DNA. As a child, I chased it. As an adult, I will learn to embrace it. I will not let regulations, rules, or rejection erase it. God created me and will help me unleash my creativity to a greater degree.

I will challenge and stretch myself and push past my comfort zones.

And when I fail, I won't feel alone.

For my identity is rooted in Christ, who awakens my soul.

I will use my talents and gifts to bring Him glory. I will engage with God throughout my creative process and let Him write the story. I will be intentional to cultivate and nurture new ideas. I will encourage others, allow myself to dream, take risks, and believe that God holds the key to unlock new possibilities. I am created to create so that people will desire to connect with and reflect the

Ultimate Creator.

CREATED TO Create

GOD SEES NOT JUST
WHO YOU ARE
BUT WHO YOU CAN BECOME.
SO HE OFFERS OPPORTUNITIES
TO USE YOUR ABILITIES
FOR HIS GLORY.

Creative Assignment

*He has filled them with skill to do all kinds of
work as engravers, designers, embroiderers in
blue, purple and scarlet yarn and fine linen, and
weavers—all of them skilled workers and designers.*

EXODUS 35:35

Years ago, I sat in a dimly lit edit bay, editing a video for a client whose company was worth billions of dollars. (No, it wasn't Bill Gates, Jeff Bezos, or Warren Buffett. Although any of those would have made for an exciting story.) Let's call this man Fancy Dude.

I knew my life experiences and objectivity could impact this piece, but in the end, I was communicating Fancy Dude's vision. It wasn't my own story to create, but he had given me ownership over it in a way. This is a similar process to the way we cocreate with God.

"Make that text bigger," he suggested.

"It's tooooo green."

"Move that sound bite to the end of the piece."

After I revised the video with Fancy Dude's inspiration, I stood up for a break. At least, I tried to. My foot got caught on the chair, and I stumbled to the ground, landing in front of his feet. There I was, five months pregnant, an Emmy® Award–winning video editor, lying on the ground as if it were company nap time. I toyed with the idea of pretending I was dramatically performing one-liners from *Nacho Libre*. Instead, I blinked away the tears and mumbled some socially awkward remark.

I was mortified and feeling all tripped up (pun intended).

Am I even good enough to be on this project? Why was I chosen to create this...

Fancy Dude met me where I was at, held out his hand, and helped me up.

How often do we feel insecure in our God assignments, wondering if we are crafty enough, smart enough, or skilled enough to do the task set before us?

But why not you? **God assigns us creative projects and wants us to have ownership of them.** Let's take a look at some biblical examples.

God gave His first creative assignment in the Garden of Eden. God partnered with Adam and brought him animals.[1] Can we just take a moment to marvel at God's amazing project-management skills? He did all the heavy lifting, hand delivering the animals one by one, and gave Adam the fun job of naming them.

Brace yourself...

"Cow."

"Chicken."

"Bear."

You've just witnessed the genius work of Adam, the first professional namer-of-things. (Yes, that's a real job.[2])

Before you ditch this book to go find a new career, let's just pause for a moment and try to give this animal a name.

This animal is named _____

It's harder than it looks, huh?

Here's the thing—God could have easily named the animals Himself.[3] Instead, **He chose to give Adam the opportunity to influence the world.**

The Bible is filled with examples of God empowering people's creativity.

STRATEGIC STORYTELLING

Thank You, Jesus, for Your parables.

Jesus creatively communicated with simple stories that illustrated valuable life lessons. From the lost sheep to the lost son, these stories teach in a way that show the Father's love.[4]

MAKING *STUFF*

Oh, and then there was that time in Genesis 6 when God told Noah some insider info about a massive flood He was sending to kill off (almost) all mankind and animals on the earth. (I'm paraphrasing, of course.) Noah played it cool and listened as God advised him how to build a 450-foot-long ark. Noah, the woodworking ninja, actually created the ark and wrangled animals into that thing![5] Talk about creative skills! I can barely sail a toy boat, let alone make one, and don't even get me started on my dog training abilities. Our beagle failed puppy training school.

CREATIVE PROBLEM SOLVING

Remember the time King Solomon had to solve the mystery of which woman was a baby stealer? Mama 1 accidentally rolled onto her baby at night and killed him. As if that poor woman didn't have enough to process, she then swapped babies with Mommy 2. Mommy 2 awoke and realized this wasn't her child. (Pretty sure this is how the saying "Save the drama for your mama" came to be.) So they brought their drama to King Solomon, who had some creative supernatural wisdom. He called for his sword and declared that he would cut the living baby in two so both women could share him. Mommy 2 spoke up because her motherly instincts kicked in, and the mystery was solved.[6] I'm not advising this shock-and-awe method of problem solving, but you have to admit...it was pretty creative.

So, fellow creative ninja, as you consider what your creative assignment is in this season, don't let your insecurity stand in the way. No matter how hard you may fall, commit to being a part of what God is doing. Remember the creative abilities of Adam, Noah, King Solomon, and Jesus. Just as He filled them, God will fill you with the skill to complete the task set before you. **You are chosen to partner with God in creative ways to influence our culture and reflect Him.** Grab God's hand—He's the best boss and coworker you'll ever have.

SIMPLE PRAYER
God, help us trust You as You guide and inspire
our creative assignments. Amen!

ART
DRAW THE WORD

Pick a random word from the list below and draw a picture of what you imagine it to be. Have fun!

Smaggler	Binxie Smish	Zoomie	Pwadum	Snorfle
	Sniffledorf	Kerfuffle	Zangers	Snuskish

YOU ARE CREATED TO CREATE
SO THAT PEOPLE WILL DESIRE TO
CONNECT WITH AND REFLECT
THE ULTIMATE CREATOR.

Designed with Purpose

The point of your life is to point to Him. Whatever you are doing, God wants to be glorified, because this whole thing is His.

FRANCIS CHAN

What's my purpose?

That's something every human desperately wants to understand and live out. Sometimes people chase after a fancy job title or house, or they find purpose in creating their next masterpiece. The problem is, once they achieve it, they can't comprehend why their heart craves more.

My senior year in college, I met with my television professor (yes, TV is a major) to discuss my final video project. It was a mini-documentary of a friend who had survived and overcome years of abuse. As my purpose for that semester came to a close, I came face-to-face with my own deep wounds.

I had a broken heart from a deceptively unhealthy relationship and was stuck in depression. And in typical procrastination fashion, I had buried those wounds by keeping myself busy on this video project.

I sat there as a wounded creative, and my professor's powerful words stung: "Do you think you're struggling through depression because the project ended and you lost your purpose?"

God used that question to help me become self-aware. I was living a purpose that was focused on me and not on Him. This revelation was life-changing for me.

MY PURPOSE WAS FOCUSED ON...	BUT MY PURPOSE SHOULD HAVE BEEN FOCUSED ON...
my job title	who can be impacted (we'll talk more about influence tomorrow)
my talents and abilities	
where I was working and the projects I was working on	who should be glorified in it

Dare I suggest that our purpose should not depend on the "what" but the "who"? **Passions and dreams can change with the seasons, but glorifying God should be our life's most persistent pursuit.** The Westminster Catechism sums it up perfectly: "Man's chief end is to glorify God and to enjoy Him forever."[1]

How do we keep that in the forefront of our minds? Let's look at the example of one American journalist—Dan Rather. He kept slips of paper in his pocket, at his desk, and in his wallet. On those little pieces of paper he had written, "Is what you are doing now helping the broadcast?"[2]

Get out a pen and paper, my friend, and write yourself this reminder:

"IS WHAT I AM DOING NOW GLORIFYING GOD?"

Stick those notes on your coffee mug, on your dashboard, and all over your space. If I had done that in college, I would have focused on my true purpose—**contentment in Christ**—rather than solely on the task at hand. Projects end and talents may fade, but the Lord's love endures forever.[3] Stay focused on the "who" and not the "what."

God has placed dreams and passions in your heart that comingle with your gifting, talents, and abilities. Have the guts to chase after those dreams and create. Write, sing, photograph, paint...and as you cocreate this masterpiece of life, may you see the endless ways you can proclaim His greatness. May that be your focus and purpose. Living from the inside out—glorifying God in the midst of the good, the bad, and the messy.

SO, FELLOW CREATIVE, WHO IS YOUR PURPOSE?

SIMPLE PRAYER
Lord, help us to glorify You in all we do. Amen!

Typography is the art of arranging text on a page.

Imagine each word having a unique voice.
Is the text trying to be heard?

Is it lost, *lighthearted*, *EXPLOSIVE*, or **BOLD**?
Pair two opposite fonts together. Examples: SERIF and SANS SERIF, **fat** and skinny.

Word size matters. Think about that as you design.

Spacing between and around the letters in each word is important.
Play with your leading, tracking, and kerning.
Arrange the words. Does the message need the words to be close together, smooshed, sideways, or spaced proportionally to effectively communicate?
If your design is too hard to read, start again!
Typography should ease the reader into understanding your message, not confuse the reader.
Remind yourself that sometimes **simpler is better!**

TRACKING

LEADING

KERNING

DIGITAL STORY
TYPOGRAPHY

    In today's challenge, you'll design a graphic for social media. By utilizing an app on your smartphone or graphic design software, write the words **Glorify and Enjoy God** using the typography tips. If you are having trouble in the digital world, feel free to grab a pencil and hand draw today's challenge.

THE BEST
CREATIVE ASSIGNMENTS
ARE FROM GOD BECAUSE
THEY HOLD HIS POWER
TO INFLUENCE.

7 Influence Culture

*Influence is a result of our love,
humility, and obedience to God,
not a goal to be achieved.*

OS HILLMAN

In 1975, Bill Bright, founder of Campus Crusade, and Loren Cunningham, founder of Youth with a Mission, developed a God-given strategy for influencing our world. Their mandate was to bring godly change to a nation by impacting its seven spheres of societal influence:[1]

In which of these spheres do you spend the most time? Circle one.

religion   family   education   government

media   arts & entertainment   business

The leaders at the top of these spheres shape the ideas and opinions of millions of others. Like them, you, too, can make an impact. **"Let your light shine before others, that they may see your good deeds and glorify your Father in heaven."**[2] Whether it's your nice-dude attitude as you find a faster way to crunch numbers or a communication breakthrough with a hard-to-reach student, you are making an impact within your sphere.

WHEN YOUR AIM IS TO GLORIFY GOD
AS YOU WALK OUT YOUR UNIQUE CALLING AND
EMBRACE THE CREATIVITY THAT GOES ALONG WITH IT,
YOU'RE SHAPING THE CULTURE.

Pray and ask God whom you can influence in your present community.

_____

_____

_____

What does being an influencer look like in the
media or arts & entertainment sphere?

_____

_____

_____

It looks like Hillary Scott as she wrote a letter to God after she suffered a miscarriage. Her heartbreak inspired her song "Thy Will," which is featured on her first solo album. She stepped into the messy place of processing her grief with God in a creative way, and out came a song fueled by heartbreak and God's redemptive power.

I read through the thousands of social media comments surrounding Hillary's song. People responded by saying they felt comforted, understood, and loved. Her song was shaping the minds of others experiencing everything from thoughts of suicide to the loss of loved ones and providing them with the courage to process their own pain.

In the things we make and our attitude when we create, we can showcase the character of God. It isn't always about the "what" you are creating, but the "who" behind it.

Writer Whitney Hopler put it this way: "If you want to make a powerful and lasting impact on the culture, you've got to do more than just consume it, critique it, condemn it or copy it. The only way to truly change the culture is to create something new for it—something that will inspire people enough to reshape their world."[3]

In our own creative processes, we need to let Holy Spirit be the main influencer. So when you create, realize that Holy Spirit is involved and wants to be a part of it. Listen to the voice of God and be obedient to the things He's placed on your heart. Holy Spirit will set things into motion as we start doing. Using our talents and gifts and embracing our creative DNA, we have opportunities to create so that people will desire to connect with and reflect the Ultimate Creator.

In what way is the content you're creating making an impact?

_____

_____

_____

TIPS & TRICKS
from an Industry Expert

MINDY RODENBURG
brand polisher in the marketing industry

When people ask you, "What do you do?" what is the first thing you think of? Is it the task you do? ("I'm a physical therapist.") Try focusing instead on the audience you serve. ("I help people recover from injury by showing them how to rebuild their strength and mobility.") By shifting the answer to mention whom you help instead of spouting off a job title, you'll create a greater impression. And each time you say it, you'll be reminding yourself just what a difference you make!

DAY 7
Creative Challenge

WRITING
WHAT DO YOU DO?

Fill in the sentence below to generate your own intro.

I _____

| *verb* | *whom you served* | *what* | *how* |
| *(action)* | *(target audience)* | *(problem solved)* | *(transformation)* |

Example: "I help small-business owners connect with who matters most to them by elevating their communication skills."

49

Thoughts or Reflections

_____
_____
_____
_____
_____
_____
_____
_____
_____
_____
_____
_____
_____
_____

8   Get Social

Congrats! You made it through act 1, The Foundation. I feel a pizza party coming on!

LET'S RECAP SOME KEY TAKEAWAYS

- God is the Ultimate Creator.
- Jesus wants to be in relationship with you.
- You are created in the image of God, which means you are creative too.
- Sin, pain, and shame can sometimes get in the way of our creative nature.
- Your purpose is to glorify and enjoy God.
- The best creative assignments are from God, because they hold His power to influence.
- Check in with your accountability partner and tell him or her all you've learned so far.

YOU ARE CREATED TO CREATE!

FREESTYLE

GET SOCIAL

Utilizing what you learned this past week, use your creative ability to share kind words with a friend or family member. First, invite Holy Spirit into your process. Pray and ask who should be the recipient of your creation. Jot down that person's name. Write down some encouraging thoughts for that person. Draw a picture, write a poem, prank call him or her with a freestyle rap, design a card...do whatever you want to creatively express your encouragement. Share your masterpiece, you creative ninja, you!

ACT 2

CREATIVITY KILLERS

BECOME SELF-AWARE
THROUGH PRAYER.

Introduction

Since we are surrounded by such a great cloud of witnesses, let us throw off everything that hinders and the sin that so easily entangles. And let us run with perseverance the race marked out for us, fixing our eyes on Jesus, the pioneer and perfecter of faith. For the joy set before him he endured the cross, scorning its shame, and sat down at the right hand of the throne of God.

HEBREWS 12:1-2

In elementary school, we participated in field days—basically, little kid Olympics. When I was in fourth grade, field days arrived with dark clouds spitting large droplets of water on our team's championship dreams. The schoolyard flooded, and the newly produced swamp stood in our way of bringing home sweet victory. The rain was so bad we could have played bucket brigade in the puddles. Not wanting to reschedule, the school moved our games inside.

My team was the Purple Dragons. We entered the gym wearing our team T-shirts and shorts. The fastest five from our class were selected for the running-rope obstacle course. We strategized how we'd run the length of the gym twice, and we fought over who would lead our squad. Since I was known for my football skills at recess, I was chosen as the closer, or as preschoolers would say, the caboose. The caboose was a coveted spot because you could see the teammates ahead of you while surveying the lay of the land. Four teammates stood in front of me holding the jump rope, dirty from missed jumps and outside play. I grabbed on, adjusting the position of my hands, knowing that if I let go, it would be over.

The whistle signaled our start. My team ran fast, dodging cones and jumping through tires. My hand slipped, but I regained composure and held that rope as tightly as a million-dollar lottery ticket. We were in the lead, but as I glanced back to see by how much, my sneaker scuffed the top of a tire and I fell. My body hit the ground just 20 feet away from the finish line.

I refused to let go. "Runnnnn!" I screamed. The four others dragged all 70 (or so) pounds of me through the rest of the obstacle course. I didn't let go until we crossed the finish line.

The race landed me in the nurse's office. My legs, arms, and hands suffered major rope and floor burns from holding the rope while being dragged across the gym floor. I was a bloody and bruised mess.

I should have let go of the rope sooner.

My question to you: How are you running your creative race? Are you holding a rope of unhealthy habits or thoughts that are slowing you down or causing damage as you move forward? Are you entangled in the rope of rejection or lies that have been yelled from the sidelines? Or are you able to let go of the rope of insecurity, failure, or comparison and run this race with perseverance and with your eyes fixed on Jesus?

I don't know about you, but **I'm so over being dragged across the finish line.** Like countless other creatives, I have the battle wounds to prove my knocked-out, dragged-across, finish-the-project-no-matter-the-cost history.

As creative ninjas, we need to overcome the obstacles that stand in our way so we can create from a healthy place.

Hebrew 12:1 says to "throw off everything that hinders and the sin that so easily entangles." Run your creative race toward Jesus and *let go of the rope* that is killing your creativity.

Sometimes we aren't even aware of these obstacles. Sometimes these obstacles are deep pain, guilt, sin, or shame. The next eight days will take us through some of the most common creativity killers.

Welcome to act 2, where we will identify and unravel character flaws and roadblocks to creativity so we can give Holy Spirit room to flow. Become self-aware through prayer. We'll walk through the process of learning to let go of the hindrances—from harmful words spoken over us to a simple lack of time—and address possible sin or sources of discouragement. We'll invite God to breathe new life into us. After all, He makes things new all the time. Let's learn to run this creative race well! **Rather than embracing creativity killers, let's start becoming creativity pursuers.**

SIMPLE PRAYER

God, help us to become self-aware through prayer and
to run toward Your redemptive power. Amen.

ART

PEN TO PAPER

Is there something you always wished you could draw but couldn't? Well, now you can! Go to YouTube and search for a basic drawing tutorial and put that pen to paper. I upped my game with online drawing lessons and moved from the girl who can't draw a stick figure to one who can now draw a horse! Miracles *do* happen! Have fun!

CREATE AFRAID.

Fee

Fear

*Holy fear is the key to God's sure foundation,
unlocking the treasures of salvation, wisdom,
and knowledge. Along with the love of God,
it composes the very foundation of life!*

JOHN BEVERE

A healthy creative identity starts with fear—but not the kind most of us fight.

Unhealthy fear can steal your creative joy or stop your pen from writing. When fear is rooted in insecurity, our thoughts and actions can be frozen in place. We shouldn't be afraid of failure, success, being wrong, wondering if it's right…But we should have a different kind of fear—the fear of the Lord. Oftentimes we have this backward. We are so afraid of the *stuff* of everyday life that we don't even try, and we miss out on the joy of obediently fulfilling our divine calling.

You are not called to fear rejection, people, failure, or the obstacles in your way. You are called to fear God. Getting this backward can be a huge creativity killer.

In Proverbs, King Solomon said, "The fear of the LORD is the beginning of knowledge, but fools despise wisdom and instruction."[1] Fearing the Lord is where greater knowledge starts. When you fear Him, you aren't petrified by the prospect of punishment. You don't think, *I better do this, or I'll get struck by lightning.*

It's a positive fear.

It's a fear motivated by love that causes you to change, grow, and understand the very power and nature of Christ. It's a fear that fuels your passion to create, knowing that He's the source of it all.

> ## FUN FACT
> The Hebrew verb *yare* can mean "to fear, to respect, to reverence," and the Hebrew noun *yirah* "usually refers to the fear of God and is viewed as a positive quality."[2]

LIE	TRUTH
I can't create because I am afraid.	I'm a God-fearing creative.

When we have a healthy fear of God, we are expressing reverent, awe-inspired submission to Him. When we are God-fearing, we are willing to push through our fear of failure and to confront the other obstacles that stand in the way. Creativity killers, like people pleasing, perfectionism, and anxiety won't be as prevalent when we revere the Lord. A creative ninja with a healthy fear of God understands who the Creator is and grasps the heartbreaking consequences of sin and disobedience. We can marvel at the power of the Ultimate Creator when we align our focus with His. We're vessels through whom His story can flow, and we're willing to grow as we create afraid.

SIMPLE PRAYER

God, help us to be creatives who "continue to work out [our] salvation with fear and trembling."[3] Amen.

CREATIVE PROCESS
MIND MAP

When brainstorming new creative projects, I start with a mind map. A mind map is a tool that helps you visualize your ideas, make free associations, and think outside the box. It also helps you to stop overanalyzing your thoughts so your ideas can flow.

Here's an example:

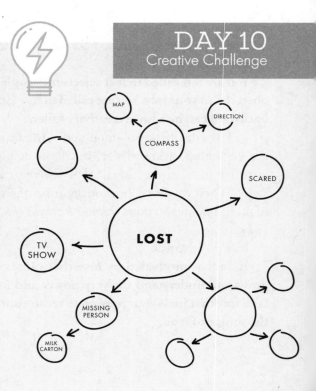

Let's try it! Hold a brainstorming session for a song you're developing titled "Shelter."

First, pray and ask Holy Spirit to inspire your brainstorming process.

Next, write the word "shelter" in a bubble in the middle of a blank page.

Now...when you think of the word "shelter," what other thoughts come to mind? There's no bad idea. Label each idea with one word in a bubble.

Invest five minutes really fleshing out this topic. In the end, you'll have different thoughts and ideas to pull from as you take the next step in creating your piece.

Put a star by your two ideas with the most potential. Save your mind map for later. (Hint: We may or may not be using it in a later challenge.)

SHELTER

IMAGINATION AND CREATIVITY
DECREASE WITH AGE.

Rules and Regulations

To fully experience our unlimited creativity, we need to return to a childlike state of play where there is a wonderment and awe at experiencing and discovering the workings and manifestation of creation.

K. FERLIC

I kept tripping over pillows and blankets on the floor as I scurried around, trying to clean up the breakfast dishes. If I hadn't seen my three-year-old daughter tearing the room apart searching for a specific pillow, I would have thought we got robbed.

"Mom, I NEEEEED THE FAN!" my five-year-old yelled from the other room.

"NO FAN! It's winter, yo!" The "yo" at the end was to prove to my kids I was the only super chill thing they needed in their life, not the blowing wind from circling plastic.

They were *always* up to something. So far our day had consisted of...

- Pretending to make a cake with Cheerios—which was followed by a mom lecture about not spilling food on the floor every day, all day.

- Arts and crafts—where I showed them how to color in the lines in a nice, structured fashion.

- Practicing their silly voices—which were too loud and squeaky.

And now the need for a fan. I was ready for nap time, and it was only nine thirty in the morning.

As I picked up a pillow and tossed it back onto the couch, I caught a glimpse of what was happening in the playroom.

In that moment, I saw their creativity, and I was crushed.

Crushed, because I was totally killing it.

Psychologist Dr. Robert Epstein says that stress and time constraints are two well-known creativity killers.[1] Add "your mama" to that list, and this was our current situation.

Their red table was turned on its side, the legs butted up to the front a chair. The chair was a sitting space for Peanut Butter Pup, one of their favorite stuffed animals. Behind the chair was a blue toy chest, spilling over with a toy giraffe, a lion, elephants, and monkeys. At the end of the toy chest was an empty space.

A space fit for a fan.

On the floor were three circular pillows propped up like wheels, leaning against the perfectly positioned rectangle they had made.

I have no idea how their tiny frames rearranged the furniture by themselves, but my kids ghetto-rigged a truck, and their dedication was impressive. It turns out this truck was broken down because of lack of materials. This truck had plans to bring their stuffed animals to the zoo, but without a fan for a motor, they couldn't go. How can a zoo survive without any animals?

I had created a disaster in their imaginary land. Can you relate to unintentionally being a major buzz kill?

Imagine an empty toy chest. It's like I plopped my kids in it and kept them in their safe little box. I was putting limitations and boundaries on their creativity simply because I was feeling tired and burned out.

IMAGINATION AND CREATIVITY DECREASE WITH AGE. I HAD JUST PROVED IT.

After a dramatic apology, we frantically searched for the fourth circular pillow-wheel, and I brought out the fan.

Who cares if they freeze their booties off? They needed this.

I needed this.

I made the choice to be present in their state of play. Their creative use of resources inspired me.

As an adult, my creativity feels different. It isn't as organic; it seems more polished and structured. My kids turned a once-empty space into something with intention and purpose in their world.

They found the fourth wheel and mounted it to its axle. The fan slipped into its waiting spot. With one turn of a button, the "motor" was on, and they zoomed off to the zoo.

When was the last time you spoke in silly
voices or colored outside the lines?

_____

_____

_____

What does God see when He looks at you?

☐ a carefree person filled with childlike awe and freedom

☐ a complicated person who colors in the lines and follows all the rules

LIE	TRUTH
I'm older, which means I'm boring and can't have fun in my creativity.	Older and wiser, I can retrain myself to embrace childlike wonder, which will strengthen my creative process.

My kids are in a constant state of play. Their imagination is always swirling, and they're always crafting, tinkering, and making *stuff*. Here I am, telling them to straighten up, follow the rules, do what I say.

If this goes on long enough, they'll be in their neat, tidy box waving bye-bye to their 98 percent of genius-level creativity in no time.

COMBAT OPPRESSIVE RULES AND REGULATIONS BY...

- knowing that creativity is in your DNA
- creating from a place of innocence and wonder
- marveling at the beauty God put in front of you, taking a leap of faith to create in an uninhibited way
- embracing what makes your creativity unique
- exploring the unknown
- asking "why" with childlike curiosity
- doing something

When you play and create with childlike innocence, you make *stuff* without fear of judgment. **Like a child, when you create in undamaged and untarnished ways, you are creating out of God's original design without rules and regulations.**

PERFORMANCE
DANCE PARTY

Pick your favorite song, turn up the beats, and host a dance party. Decide not to care about who's watching or judging your moves. The goal is to have fun, feel free, and be silly. Bonus points if you do the worm across the floor.

Reflect on how you felt.

Then, don't forget to check off this challenge on the contents page.

YOU AREN'T CALLED TO
BE A TORTURED ARTIST;
YOU ARE CALLED TO BE
ENTHRALLED BY
THE THRONE OF GRACE.

Tortured Artist

Let us come boldly to the throne of our gracious God. There we will receive His mercy, and we will find grace to help us when we need it most.

HEBREWS 4:16 NLT

Have you ever met the tortured artist types? Perhaps wearing all black with the smell of alcohol haunting their days? Paint is under their fingernails because they forgot to shower again as their demons haunted them throughout the night. They speak in poetic rhymes and eloquent quips but fail to communicate in their relationships. Depression and anxiety lurk around them, often found in the deep thoughts that appear on the pages in their novels. They suffer in solitude with the pieces of their broken hearts lost in the darkness. Their vibe is often mellow yet eccentric and (some might say) "crazy." Often, they have unknowingly welcomed sin into their creativity. Afraid to search for peace of mind, fearing their creativity will flee, tortured artists often feel lonely.

Without peace, a troubled mind struggles through constant torment.

Of course, I'm stereotyping the tortured artist. But in my college years, I could have been labeled as one. I was stuck in my own depression and anxiety. My pain and broken heart were overwhelming, and I lost my creative passion.

Globally, more than 300 million people of all ages suffer from depression.[1] At its worst, it can lead to the fate of Robin Williams, Kurt Cobain, and Ernest Hemingway—suicide. These deaths are tragedies, and the artists' creativity is documented only in movies, music, and writings. Not in living, breathing lives.

I often hear celebrities say that great art comes from our brokenness. I disagree. **Research has proven that people are most creative when they are in a positive mood.**[2] As we discussed briefly in day 7, great art can come from great pain *when* we find the good in it. True creativity flourishes not in darkness, but in light. We'll tackle that thought more in an upcoming lesson on redemptive vulnerability.

LIE	TRUTH
I'm called to be a tortured artist.	I'm called to be enthralled by the throne of grace.

IF YOUR CREATIVE IDENTITY IS ENTRENCHED IN DEPRESSION, I HUMBLY CHALLENGE YOU TO…

- Get help! Tell a trusted pastor, counselor, doctor, family member, or friend.
- Fight this battle with Christ and trust that you can get to the other side of it.
- Understand that healing is almost always a process.
- Ask for prayer and get in community.
- Ask God to forgive you for accepting this whole tortured artist vibe. Don't declare that over yourself!

"The righteous cry out, and the Lord hears them; he delivers them from all their troubles."[3] Sometimes healing comes in an instant; often, it's a process. For me, it was a journey of counseling, community, prayer, coloring books, and focusing on gratitude for all God was doing in my life. For others, the battle is lifelong.

If you are struggling in the darkness, my prayer is that you have greater perseverance and strength today.

> "Anxiety does not empty tomorrow of its sorrows, but only empties today of its strength."
>
> Charles Spurgeon

SIMPLE PRAYER

Lord, we lift up all the creative ninjas who struggle with depression, whether they are famous or known only by You. Holy Spirit, shower them with greater joy, peace, and love. Give them the courage to fight! Amen.

ART

COLORING ISN'T JUST FOR KIDS

Phew—today's lesson was heavy! Let's de-stress with today's kid-friendly challenge.

Adult coloring books are all the rage these days. For more than a decade, researchers and art therapists alike have promoted the calming benefits of coloring. Grab your colored pencils and turn to one of the full-sized coloring sheets (pages 14, 37, 67, 89, 101, 115, 149). Have fun!

DITCH YOUR BAD ATTITUDE
FOR SOME GRATITUDE.

13

Stress

You are the only Bible some unbelievers will ever read, and your life is under scrutiny every day.

JOHN MACARTHUR

Swoooooosh.

Zingggggg.

Shhhhhhooooooooo.

Swweeeeeeeeeeee.

I was editing a behind-the-scenes look into an animated film. We were just days away from our project's due date as I hunted for the perfect sound effect to accommodate the studio's notes.

I had on my typical editor uniform—flip-flops, jeans, and a zipped-up hoodie sweatshirt.

When the hoodie was up, I was in video editor's paradise and should not be interrupted because magic was happening. It's Edit Bay Etiquette 101, people. So there I am, hoodie up, in the zone. The *swoooosh* was in its proper place as I played back what we had created.

I pored over days of footage and interviews from the film's masterminds. My producer and I worked together to show how the filmmakers translated the beauty of Africa into the style of their film. This project birthed a dream inside me to take an African safari. I can picture it now—cruising in a jeep, chasing wildebeests, wearing my khaki pants and green safari shirt, mosquito repellent wafting through the wind...

And suddenly it was gone. The lions and African plains flickered, and then the screen went black.

I ran through some routine computer troubleshooting techniques, but they produced no results, only disappointment.

Everything was gone. *Everything.*

I wanted to road rage against my computer and throw it through the window, but all I could do was put my head on my desk and cry. Hundreds of hours of work gone due to a faulty external server. This was the company's biggest tech crash to date and has since been dubbed The Crash of '07.

This moment was one of the most stressful in my Hollywood editing career, and there was no easy way to fix it. We had to completely rebuild the video.

Hopefully this question won't bring up some post-traumatic stress for you, but imagine your last stressful situation at work or school.

How did you respond when stress hit?

My unhealthy stress response looks something like this:

- Cry or grumble around
- Grab some chocolate or a Diet Pepsi
- Tell jokes

What are your unhealthy response methods?

Stress is a normal part of life, and there are helpful and unhelpful ways to deal with it. I had to ditch my bad attitude for some gratitude and figure out a way around this situation. We can't ditch a stressful life, but we can learn how to handle life's pressures by depending on God.

Our mind is often the troublemaker. The prophet Isaiah shows us a better way: "You will keep in perfect peace those whose minds are steadfast, because they trust in you."[1]

Healthy stress responses often include slowing down, praying, and asking God to help you.

Learn to rest in His peace when stress hits. When you do, you clear your mind from the stress and make space for creative and innovative ideas.

What could your healthy responses to stress look like?

_____

_____

_____

_____

So there we were, tired and smelly but in good spirits as a team, and I sat in the edit bay rebuilding everything that had taken months to create. We worked three days straight, creatively solving problems and recreating what we had lost. I was fueled by Diet Pepsi and Jesus, and we met our deadline.

The lesson here isn't about being the company hero or a tech wizard. It's about responding to an out-of-control situation in healthy ways that honor God and honor people. Months later, on my last day at work before transitioning out of this job, a coworker said something to me that I will never forget.

"YOU MADE ME BELIEVE IN JESUS."

I'm not telling you this story so you'll send me on a trip to Africa because I'm soooo awesome. I'm a hot mess. I wanted to throw my computer out the window, remember? But time and again, God helped me seize an opportunity to rely on Him for strength and wisdom while navigating a stressful situation. The peace I learned to carry in the workplace chaos demonstrated the character of Christ—and my coworker noticed.

LIE	TRUTH
Stress should be nonexistent in my world.	Stress happens. Carrying God's peace during chaos can demonstrate the character of Christ.

We all have the power to turn our frown upside down. The next time stress creeps in as you tackle a creative project, let it go and continue your flow. Rely on Holy Spirit for peace and seize the opportunity to let God work through you.

SIMPLE PRAYER
Lord, help us lean into You when we are in stressful situations. Amen!

JESSIE JOY
worship leader

3 KEY ELEMENTS TO HAVE IN PLACE BEFORE WRITING A WORSHIP SONG

1. **Spend time in God's presence.** Get to know Him intimately and connect with His heart through time alone in prayer and worship.

2. **Spend time in the Word learning about His character.** Reading the Psalms is a great way to start getting to know who God is—His loving-kindness, goodness, faithfulness...even His power, wrath, and might.

3. **Learn to recognize when you're about to "birth" a song.** You feel an urgency in your heart when a song is stirring inside. Discipline yourself to sit down with a pen and paper and start writing from an overflow of a heart that's connecting with God.

FUN FACT

Reading Scripture to find God's attributes and actions is known as the theocentric method of Bible study because it makes God the center of our attention.

WRITING

WORSHIP SONG

Apply Jessie's tips and tricks in today's challenge. Invite Holy Spirit into your writing process as you write the lyrics to a chorus for a worship song. The working title is "Shelter." Review your mind map from day 10. Grab your Bible and meditate on Psalm 91. Whether it's a word, phrase, verse, or thought, write it down as you begin to piece together the chorus for "Shelter." If you are using this devotional with friends, feel free to collaborate. Have fun!

SERVE OTHERS CREATIVELY
WITH A PASSION TO
PLEASE GOD, NOT PEOPLE.

People Pleasing

Am I now trying to win the approval of human beings, or of God? Or am I trying to please people? If I were still trying to please people, I would not be a servant of Christ.

GALATIANS 1:10

You're talking with a friend who says, "I know you have crazy creative skills and your talents are in hot demand. So I was wondering if you could..."

Were you thinking *yes* even before your friend finished the sentence?

When I first moved to Hollywood, I went through a season of *yes*. The projects were exciting, I began serving in the local church, and my schedule was jam-packed with new adventures. "Why, yes, I'll edit your video for free all night long so I can 'build my résumé.' Oh, and you need a ride to LAX during rush hour? No problem. I'll grab a coffee for you with my nonexistent money."

I hope they like me.

I hope my servant-hearted ways brings them happiness.

Over time, my desire to serve others and glorify God with my talents shifted. I went from pleasing God to pleasing people. Sometimes I really wanted my yes to be a no, but I didn't want to let people down or disappoint them.

It was as if I were driving down a road headed toward my exit, but along came a person who *desperately* needed my help. Clearly, I was the only one to save him. We linked arms and took a detour. I ended up in side streets, dark alleyways, and back roads. I was being pulled in a million directions, and none of them were taking me to my exit. I was poor, late, and really tired, and I had nothing left to give.

When your yes feels like that, your servant heart and sacrifice have been hijacked, and you are attempting to win the approval of others by people pleasing. You are no longer glorifying God, but idolizing man.

LIE	TRUTH
My value comes from other people's praise.	My value comes from my identity in Christ.

When I took on whatever came my way, I was glorifying myself, not God. I craved the affirmations others gave, and I hated disappointing them by saying no to their requests. In my season of yes, I had an unhealthy perspective. I wasn't valuing my time and energy, and I got stuck in people pleasing and a performance mentality.

PEOPLE-PLEASING WAYS CAN…

- affect your relationship with God
- strain your family
- affect your ability to make wise decisions
- take a toll on your mental and physical health

Ask yourself this: *Is my motivation to create stuff driven by people or by God?*

If you're constantly saying yes to requests you don't actually want or feel called to fulfill, you may be a people pleaser. My yes was draining my energy, and my people-pleasing ways were killing my creativity.

As with everything, seasons come and go, and so will your seasons of saying yes or no. If you're in a season of having time to take more on, consider whether you are saying yes because you want (or even need) to make others happy, or you are truly feeling like God wants you to give it your all. Then do what you know is right!

HOW TO SET HEALTHY BOUNDARIES

- Ask God to help you know when to tackle the request and when to say no.
- Realize you have a choice. Sometimes a no is better for you, your personal goals, or your family.
- Get comfortable saying yes and saying no. Set your priorities. Make a list of the things you want to focus on today or this week. This will help you keep focused on the things that do matter.

Author Matt Chandler thinks of it like this: **"Your approval before God is woven into the life and sacrifice of Jesus Christ on the cross, not what other men and women think about you."**[1] Knowing my approval comes from God, I've had the freedom to chase new and creative adventures without being bound by the shackles of people's approval. The times I froze mid-adventure were the times I caught myself wondering, *What will people think?*

My creativity was stalled the second I began chasing the approval of others rather than resting in the approval of God.

Once I became self-aware, Holy Spirit took me through a season of saying no to many of the things I once craved.

What would it look like if we just let go of our longing for the approval of others and lived fully surrendered to the One? I believe we'd be bigger risk-takers. I believe we'd sense Holy Spirit directing our lives and learn to follow the gentle voice of God instead of the conflicting voices of others. Our faith would grow deeper and bolder, and we'd live fully surrendered lives. Then we'd create from the overflow.

SIMPLE PRAYER

Lord, help us to create to glorify You. May we get our affirmation from You, not from serving others. Amen.

DIGITAL STORY

DAY 14
Creative Challenge

MEMORIES

By utilizing an app on your smartphone, graphic design software, or markers or colored pencils, create a graphic representing a special memory. Think of a moment you had with God that significantly impacted your life. Recreate an element of that moment in artistic form. For example, if the memory happened at the beach, create a color palette inspired by the ocean. Any part of that moment can be captured graphically. Describe that special memory and then turn it into a graphic design.

BE PRODUCTIVE
IN YOUR PASSION.

Time

To those who use well what they are given, even more will be given, and they will have an abundance. But from those who do nothing, even what little they have will be taken away.

MATTHEW 25:29 NLT

When you consider chasing your creative, God-given dreams, do you feel...

- ⬤ Too busy and overbooked?
- ⬤ Like a lazy or scared procrastinator?
- ◯ Like you're waiting for the perfect moment?
- ◯ Like giving a high-five because you're doing it?

Mismanaging your time can be a huge creativity killer.

I'm going to be fully vulnerable for a minute. Before I became a video editor or speaker, these things were all just God-given dreams.

I'm a recovering procrastinator, and my creativity flows into the late hours of the night. Often tired, I had no trouble finding something "better" to monopolize my time...*Gilmore Girls,* anyone? How about scrolling through social media for the umpteenth time? Aimless "interneting" can be the biggest distraction to pursuing our dreams.

Until one day when I stopped procrastinating and started doing. You know the saying "You make time for the things you value"? When I started placing value on my God-given dreams, I began to act with creative courage. As I learned to be more productive in my passion, God strengthened my craft and expanded my areas of influence.

HERE'S WHAT I LEARNED

1. **Write stuff down.** Turn those goals into small, actionable items. Focus on tangible things you can easily check off your list. The items won't overwhelm you, so you will be able to pursue them with confidence. Here's an example.

   Bad actionable goal: Write a 250-page book.
   Good actionable goal: Map out an outline for a book by Thursday.

2. **Realize you'll always be busy.** Be intentional about carving out a certain amount of time each day to focus on your creative goals. Start at five minutes. Understand that there is never a perfect time to create. Sometimes you'll have to hold a meeting in the car while driving the kids to school or practice a freestyle rap while making breakfast.

3. **Set priorities and deadlines.** In the evening, make a list of the things you want to accomplish the next day. This will help you keep focused on the things that matter for you in this season. Then have the determination and drive to stick to the list!

4. **Remove distractions.** When it's time to work, hide your phone, turn off the internet, and remove the other distractions that cause you to shift your focus from your main thing.

5. **Be flexible.** Sometimes God has another plan for your schedule that day. Be open to Holy Spirit's prompting if He takes you in another direction. Your family, your friends, or a random stranger may need you. Trust God to redeem the lost time, and chase the adventure of being led by Him.

Do you want to start a business? Write a book? Develop healthy relationships? What is your creative dream?

_____

_____

_____

LIE	TRUTH
I don't have any time in my day.	I have 1,440 minutes every day to use on the things I value.

We make time for the things we value most. Pray and ask God to help you manage your time and schedule. When I got into public speaking, I had two preschoolers. The best advice I ever received was to hold my schedule loosely and be obedient to what I felt God was asking of me minute by minute. Some days, I feel prompted to focus on ministry goals. On other days, I sense that it needs to be Legos and my kiddos.

> "Whoever can be trusted with very little can also be trusted with much." LUKE 16:10

What can you do right now, in this moment, to make the most of what you've been given? Over time, as you are faithful with the little things day in and out, you'll step back and see how God has been crafting the pieces to your big dream.

TIPS & TRICKS
from an Industry Expert

JEREMY ADAMS
Hollywood screenwriter and producer

THE TWO MOST VALUABLE THINGS YOU CAN DO TO BECOME A BETTER WRITER

1. **You need to read.** It doesn't matter if it's a screenplay, a book, or a comic book. Never stop reading! It's important to look at how other people have developed their craft and have put it out there so you can develop your craft as well.

2. **You have to find time to write.** It can be super hard—trust me, I know! So whether it's five minutes or ten minutes, the thing that will separate you from a wannabe writer or a bad writer is the fact that you put in the time to finish writing.

DAY 15
Creative Challenge

CREATIVE PROCESS

READ

Take Jeremy's advice and make time to read for five minutes. (No, this devotional doesn't count.) What did you read?

PERFECTIONISTS FIXATE ON MAKING
FLAWLESS ART, BUT OUR
GREATEST PURSUIT IS TO FIND
GOD'S PERFECT HEART.

16

Perfectionism

Understanding the difference between healthy striving and perfectionism is critical to laying down the shield and picking up your life. Research shows that perfectionism hampers success. In fact, it's often the path to depression, anxiety, addiction and life paralysis.

BRENÉ BROWN

Today's lesson is going to be extremely short because it's simple and I want it to stick. **You will never be perfect here on this earth.**

Drop the mic because that's gold.

You can develop your craft and skills, but don't get hung up on expressing your creativity perfectly. Perfectionists fixate on making flawless art, but our greatest pursuit is to find God's perfect heart.

LIE	**TRUTH**
The things I create need to be perfect.	I won't let the need for perfection stifle my creative process.

Don't let the desire for perfectionism keep you from starting the things God has placed on your heart. You'll never create the perfect painting, graphic, or video...but you can strive to be divinely inspired in your process.

SIMPLE PRAYER

Lord, help us ditch our desire for perfectionism so we can freely create. Amen.

ARIANA BROOKSHIER
natural light portrait photographer

LIGHTING TIPS TO HELP YOU TAKE BETTER PORTRAITS

1. **If you are indoors, try to use available window light.** Face your subject toward the window, but make sure the light is even on her face.

2. **Learn to work with the light in a creative way.** You can use sun and shadows to create dramatic portraits. Or if the sun is shining directly on your subject, have him pose creatively. That way, he won't just be squinting and smiling at the camera.

3. **If you're outdoors, try to find the shade.** You can also move your subject toward the shade of a wall or building. This way, you can ensure there are no patches of sunlight on the face.

4. **Learn to work with what you have.** A good photo can be taken with any type of camera if you know how to use light to your advantage. I rarely use flash, and I definitely try not to use it in any of my portraits. I'd love to challenge you to try the same in today's exercise!

PHOTOGRAPHY

DAY 16
Creative Challenge

LIGHTING

Use Ariana's lighting techniques to take a portrait. Represent the word "imperfect" in the photo. Get creative and have fun!

YOU CAN'T
OUTPERFORM GOD.

Performance Mentality

Faith is the realization that God's pleasure in you will never be based upon your performance for Him. Instead, God's pleasure in you will always be based upon Christ's performance for you.

DAVID PLATT

We live in a fast-paced culture that's constantly moving. "Hustle" is cool-kid slang for work hard and keep up. From the beginning, we're trained to chase the American dream. Hustle for straight As in your school days, prove yourself on set so you can get a promotion, overwork yourself as you write a beautiful song so people will see your talent...

In high school, I had a performance mentality. I thought that the more I did, the better I was. At one point, my guidance counselor was shocked by the five-page extracurricular activities sheet attached to my college application...she acted as if it may be an overkill. *No way,* I thought. *That's who I am.* My self-worth was derived from titles, positions, and praises from others.

Then I met Jesus...and that performance mentality wormed its way into my relationship with Him.

In my twenties, I was working a full-time editing job in the heart of Hollywood and serving as a video director in a local church. I was burned out and exhausted. One night I found myself crying outside the church doors. I remember feeling heartbroken because I felt called into ministry and the entertainment industry, but I was just so worn out, like smelly, mismatched socks with holes in the toes.

Have you ever felt that way?

I had been sucked back into a performance mentality. I was thinking the more I served in the church, the more I was earning approval in the Kingdom. The more I did, the more I was earning the love of people...and they would see that I *was* enough. The longer I read my Bible, the more God would love me.

As it turns out, you can't outperform God or earn His love. "God saved you by His grace when you believed. And you can't take credit for this; it is a gift from God. Salvation is not a reward for the good things we have done, so none of us can boast about it."[1]

A performance mentality shifts your focus from Christ. Let's look in the Bible at a story of two sisters, Mary and Martha, whose faith looked very different.

> "As Jesus and his disciples were on their way, he came to a village where a woman named Martha opened her home to him. She had a sister called Mary, who sat at the Lord's feet listening to what he said. But Martha was distracted by all the preparations that had to be made. She came to him and asked, 'Lord, don't you care that my sister has left me to do the work by myself? Tell her to help me!'
>
> 'Martha, Martha,' the Lord answered, 'you are worried and upset about many things, but few things are needed—or indeed only one. Mary has chosen what is better, and it will not be taken away from her.'"
>
> LUKE 10:38-42

KEY THINGS TO REMEMBER FROM THIS PASSAGE

- Martha was distracted with performance and seemed to be looking for praise for her hard work.
- Jesus doesn't say Martha's activities were bad, but He sees her heart and cares that she seems anxious.
- Mary took the initiative to sit at the feet of Jesus.
- Choosing to sit at the feet of Jesus is a better choice.
- Seek His presence instead of performing for Him.
- Performance mentality can leave you feeling like Martha. The more distractions that pile up, the more you pull yourself out of intimacy with Christ.

I feel ya, Martha, I've been there.

As I sat outside the church overwhelmed and distracted, I paused for a moment. Holy Spirit showed me I'd been missing this beautiful place of solidarity. **In the place of rest, we can find community and unity with Christ.** Inspiration and rejuvenation. This was a place where my soul desperately needed to be, and I desired to be reconnected to the Author of life. I needed to learn to sit at the feet of Jesus again and seek His presence instead of performing for Him.

Have you found yourself stuck in this vortex of go-go-go, attempting to prove your worth? Have you felt pulled in a million different directions, worried, weary, or upset?

LIE	**TRUTH**
I must do more to prove I am enough.	By God's grace, I am enough.

Your creative assignment doesn't define you, and neither do your failures and successes! As you are creating something new, remember that you can do it while resting in grace rather than striving to prove yourself. Busyness doesn't equal godliness. In fact, Jesus said, "Come to Me, all of you who are weary and carry heavy burdens, and I will give you rest."[2] **Performance mentality is about you proving your worth. Resting in Christ is understanding His grace in your life.**

SIMPLE PRAYER

God, help us to ditch our performance mentality, which
causes anxiety, and to seek Your presence. Amen.

ART

FINISH THIS PICTURE

Extend this squiggle into a drawing.
Snap a picture of your drawing and post it on social media with **#courageouscreative**.

Thoughts or Reflections

Get Social

18

Hooray! You made it through act 2, Creativity Killers! Now you're ready to become a creativity pursuer.

LET'S RECAP SOME KEY TAKEAWAYS

- Fearing the Lord will help you create.
- When we play and create with childlike innocence, we make *stuff* without fear of judgment.
- You're not called to be a tortured artist. You're called to be enthralled by the throne of grace.
- You can't ditch a stressful life, but you can learn how to handle life's pressures by being content in Christ.
- Serve others creatively with a passion to please God, not people.
- Your value doesn't come from other people's praise. You are valuable because of who you are in Christ.
- You have 1,440 minutes every day to use on the things you value.
- Perfectionists fixate on making flawless art, but our greatest pursuit is to find God's perfect heart.

BY GOD'S GRACE, YOU ARE ENOUGH.

FREESTYLE

GET SOCIAL

Become present with those around you—their languages, cultures, concerns, and struggles. Collaborate with Holy Spirit to transform the way you perceive those things so you see them as positive, hopeful, creative expressions.

Is your brother feeling overwhelmed by a broken relationship? Paint something that displays two mended hearts. Is your neighbor feeling grieved by racial tension? Write a poem that declares unity and promise by looking for God's heart in the situation. These are examples of prophetic art. Your goal is to express encouragement, comfort, and strength in a situation so it can be seen in a new way.

Spend some time praying and asking God whom you can create for. If you feel led, complete the project and share it.

ACT 3

UNLEASH CREATIVITY

LIVE OUT CREATIVE FREEDOM.

19

Introduction

In the first act, get your principal character up a tree; in the second act, throw stones at him; in the third, get him down gracefully.

UNKNOWN

Welcome to the third act in this book—the section devoted to "getting you down gracefully." We've ditched the creativity killers of sin, shame, guilt, and pain and are ready to become creativity pursuers. Perhaps in act 2, Holy Spirit helped you to stop entertaining the lies that have been spoken over you. Maybe your focus is no longer on pleasing people but pleasing Him. Are you ready to jump into act 3 and start unleashing creativity? This part of the story will help you understand your creative DNA and prepare to live out your creative freedom.

Stay focused on the "who" behind why you create and give yourself permission to entertain new thoughts, innovations, and dreams. Hopefully, you are no longer wandering in the uncreative wilderness like the Israelites with their disbelief.[1]

Another kind of wandering can be a good thing...

According to former Apple CEO Steve Jobs, walking can spark your creativity. He was known for his "long walks, which he used for exercise, contemplation, problem solving, and even meetings."[2] In 2014, Stanford researchers found that "walking boosts creative inspiration...A person's creative output increased by an average of 60 percent when walking."[3]

Sometimes creative inspiration happens in an instant, and sometimes it develops from routines that create space and stability and foster new ideas. Either way, your creativity can be influenced by the presence of Holy Spirit. In the final act, we'll learn to unleash our creativity by developing healthy, creative habits and mindsets, and we'll gracefully walk in obedience.

SIMPLE PRAYER
Lord, remind us daily that we are created to create. Amen!

CREATIVE PROCESS

GENIUS WALK

Go for a walk in silence.

Let your mind wander, and write down all the things you think about.

Then check off this challenge on the contents page.

CREATIVITY IS LIKE A MUSCLE;
IT MUST BE STRETCHED AND
PUSHED PAST ITS COMFORT ZONE.

20 Cultivate Your Creativity

*Amateurs sit and wait for inspiration,
the rest of us just show up and go to work.*

CHUCK CLOSE

Have I told you the story of how this book came to be?

In May 2016, I launched a small creativity course online where 32 people—some strangers, some friends—committed to making *stuff*.

Scientific evidence shows we can nurture and cultivate our creativity by retraining our minds to let it happen. Creativity is like a muscle; it must be challenged, stretched, and pushed past its comfort zone.

That was the goal of the course.

We all did the same creative activities for 31 days straight. One day, we designed graphics; the next, we gave a monologue. Together, we shared our failures and successes, and we even collaborated on writing a worship song.

At the end of the month, I surveyed the participants, and every single person who responded said that his or her creativity grew. It was as if we were exploding with new ideas and couldn't shut them off.

Six months later, this book was birthed out of that month of creativity.

Many years ago, a 15-year-old who believed in her dreams begged her mama to enroll her in a New York City drama school. She was eager to cultivate her creative talent, but her nerves got in the way in acting class. The teacher finally wrote a note home saying, "[She's] wasting her time and ours. She's too shy and reticent to put her best foot forward."[1]

Just imagine for a minute if that person let those words stick to her and define her. If she had held on to that label, her creativity could easily have been killed. But she didn't. This young girl continued to cultivate her craft and became one of America's most beloved comedians.

Lucille Ball overcame her creativity killers and continued to stretch herself. She played the iconic lead role in *I Love Lucy* and later became the first woman to run a major television production studio.

Oftentimes, we allow people to define or limit our actions. It reminds me of a young man I met who felt called to be an actor, but his dad told him, "Actors are a dime a dozen." His dad's words redefined his destiny. The ropes of insecurity and doubt were entangling him to the point of being stuck. In contrast, Lucille Ball let go of that rope of negativity and chased after the things she felt called to be.

MORE WAYS TO CONTINUE CULTIVATING YOUR CREATIVITY

- Sing it out like *Frozen* and just "Let It Go!" Continue to check in with Holy Spirit to help you ditch those creativity killers that have been spoken over you or are holding you back.

- Continue to do creative challenges in this book...and lurk around the internet for more!

- Look for opportunities to foster your talents and make yourself better! Take a painting, acting, or pottery class.

- Think of something you're really bad at (mine would be cooking) and sign up for a class or YouTube your way to learning that skill. *Bye-bye, frozen pizzas.*

- Stay committed. Realize that there will never be the perfect magical moment to cultivate your creativity, and make a point to be intentional.

- Stop making excuses.

In the famous motivational words from Shia LaBeouf and Nike, "Just do it!"

The other day, the basement of our house was flooding because our foundation was messed up. (That's as technical as I get, people.) Our basement is basically a pit of creepiness with rock walls and mass quantities of spiders. Now they are wet spiders.

I elected my creative fixer-upper husband to work his ninja skills. Five hours later (about 90 percent through the basement project), he realized he could have used a much simpler and quicker method to block the leaking wall. His hard work had sparked his creativity, opening the way to fresh ideas and a new solution.

Sometimes instead of just racking your brain for the perfect idea before you get started, or holding another brainstorming meeting on the whiteboard with your team for the thirty-second time, you just have to **get started**, and the genius solutions will come. Be obedient and start doing. From a spiritual perspective, there's no such thing as procrastinated obedience...that's just disobedience.

> "The loafer says, 'There's a lion on the loose! If I go out I'll be eaten alive!'"
>
> PROVERBS 22:13 MSG

Remember, great things don't come from laziness, what-ifs, comfort zones, or excuses. Creativity flows in the stillness of the everyday and in the intentionality of the chase. Sometimes your comfort zone can be your biggest obstacle.

Okay, I'm preaching to myself—next time I'll go into the basement.

I believe we all have gifts and abilities that can catapult us into our destiny. But before that, we often go through a season of preparation. **Cultivating your creativity will strengthen your muscle for right now and for things to come.** When Holy Spirit says go, you can flex that creative muscle and affect your sphere of influence for Jesus.

ART
EVERYDAY ITEMS

Bring an everyday item to life by blending it into a simple sketch. Snap a picture of your sketch and post it on social media using **#courageouscreative**.

*Examples by
Matt Randle*

AUTHENTICITY IS
WHAT SETS
YOUR ART APART.

Release Your Uniqueness

Be yourself;
everyone else is already taken.

OSCAR WILDE

The odds of...

- Dating a millionaire: 1 in 215[1]

- Being injured by a toilet: 1 in 10,000[2]

- Being born in this particular time, place, and circumstance: about 1 in 400,000,000,000,000[3]

Millionaire dates and toilet injuries can't compare to you! In a TEDx talk, Mel Robbins quoted research showing we had a 1 in 400 trillion chance of being born. I was awed. Awed by the hand of God, who knows every hair on my head and who "created my inmost being."[4] **Just take a moment to imagine all the things God had to orchestrate throughout history so you could be breathing in this moment.**

"You created my inmost being;
    you knit me together in my mother's womb.
I praise you because I am fearfully and wonderfully made;
    your works are wonderful,
    I know that full well."

PSALM 139:13-14

It's safe to say God created a miracle when He designed you. In the womb, you were being uniquely formed. Your unique fingerprints began to develop around 10 weeks of gestation. After 17 weeks, they were completely developed.[5] Pretty amazing, huh?

Your personality, style, beliefs, aspirations, goals, creativity, talents, appearance, gender, childhood, culture, quirks, health, intellect, speech, life events, supernatural experiences...they all make up who you are. Why do we so often fall into the trap of insecurity, uncertainty, or not valuing our God-created uniqueness?

Say hello to the comparison game.

When I interned in Los Angeles during a semester at school, my friends and I attended a seminar about living in Hollywood. The woman leading the session taught us what grocery store to go to (Ralphs) and how to track celebrities (there are tours for that), and she gave advice on fitting into the entertainment industry. She stressed the importance of having blond hair, fake nails, fake tans, and fake b…well, you get the point. She basically advised conforming to a plastic, Barbie-esque image. My friends and I left feeling defeated; we wanted to make it in this town but didn't seem to fit the mold.

In the comparison game, I got stuck thinking that in order to do the things God had placed on my heart, I needed to look or act a certain way. *Well, that person is embracing a similar calling to mine, so I should be like him or her.*

I went with this theory for a season. That person over there was highly successful in the entertainment industry, and she wore suits, used fancy words, and actually brushed her hair.

Here's the problem—jeans are considered high-class for me, big words are confusing, and I secretly wanted my dreads back. I tried to pretend I was classy by wearing heels and upgrading from Jenny to Jennifer. Somehow, people quickly found out about my false identity.

I got sucked into the comparison game and lost my unique voice.

When I was attempting to be like someone else, it was harder to stand back up after a failure because my foundation was wobbly from the start. **I wasn't feeling free to be me; I was coveting what others seemed to be.**

In Brené Brown's book *Rising Strong*, she puts it this way: "Stay in your own lane. Comparison kills creativity and joy."[6]

Talk about a punch to the gut. How can you creatively express yourself when you're too busy swerving all over the road looking at everyone else?

So what does it look like to fully embrace *you* in a healthy, wholehearted, God-honoring way?

In my twenties, God took me through a process of truly understanding who I am…and learning to be comfortable in it. Sometimes you have to fight to establish healthy identity in Christ. We'll talk more about identity in a few days, but for now, let's focus on how greatly loved and uniquely made you are. "We are God's masterpiece. He has created us anew in Christ Jesus, so we can do the good things He planned for us long ago."[7]

You are a proven miracle and a masterpiece…so own it! Not in an arrogant way, but in a way that glorifies God. **You have unique gifts, and the world needs your perspective, your passion, and your talent.** Embracing your uniqueness—whether it's your smarts, quirkiness, or aspirations—can help you understand your role as a child of God.

Art and creative expression are deeply rooted in the way you see and interact with the world. Be authentic in your interactions so Holy Spirit can use you. As you release your uniqueness to the world around you, you'll discover a God-found confidence to create afraid and do hard things.

When you can create from confidence in who God created you to be, your voice will captivate and intrigue those around you. **Authenticity is what sets your art apart.** Unleash your creativity as you release your uniqueness in today's creative challenge.

SIMPLE PRAYER
Lord, equip us to release our creative uniqueness in powerful ways! Amen.

TIPS & TRICKS
from an Industry Expert

MICHELLE CUTHRELL
author, speaker, and orphan advocate

A voice is to a writer or speaker what a unique style is to an artist. No one has to tell you that a Rembrandt is a Rembrandt or a Picasso is a Picasso. The artist has consistently delivered content over a period of time in a unique way that allows you to identify that artist's style.

The same principle applies to your voice.

You are the only one in the history of the world who speaks, writes, and thinks exactly the way you do. Others may deliver similar content or use a similar style, but you are the only one who writes and speaks in a specific way using the intonations, phrasing, pace, and style that you do.

This is your voice, and this is what makes you unique.

In this age of multimedia—whether you are a writer who needs to speak or a speaker who needs to write or an introverted artist who needs to use social media to get the word out about your awesome work—you need a voice. Everyone needs a voice.

So write like you speak and speak like you write. Blog like you write and use social media like you speak. Soon, your beautiful, unique voice will emerge. People will identify your product, not by your profile, not by your byline, not even by your fabulous face, but by your voice.

DAY 21
Unleash Creativity

WRITING
FIND YOUR VOICE

Craft a short bio describing your awesome self in 25 words or less. Think about your personality, style, beliefs, aspirations, goals, creativity, talents, appearance, childhood, culture, quirks, health, intellect, speech, life events, and supernatural experiences.

ENGAGE IN COMMUNITY WITH
CREATIVES WHERE YOU COMMISERATE
IN THE HARD, COLLABORATE
WHEN CALLED, AND CELEBRATE
ALL CHRIST IS DOING.

Engage in Community

Encourage each other and build each other up, just as you are already doing.

1 THESSALONIANS 5:11 NLT

Imagine a blank canvas.

The artist steps back and dips the brush into blue paint, hurls it at the canvas, and watches the color spread. It seems lonely, so the master painter adds yellow, more blue, blacks, greens, pinks, and reds to the canvas. Big paint blobs, little splatters, imperfect circles, messy edges. Some of the colors blend together to create something new, and others fall off the canvas and onto the floor. It feels like a mess is happening, but something special is being created.

As the paint dries, it unifies. The painter steps back to see the creation. It's a hodgepodge of uniqueness that melded together to create something beautiful.

This is what creating community looks like.

A big, messy, beautiful, splattered painting.

I want to tell you a story about one of my college friends, Pete. We bonded in our TV class over Britney Spears and dinosaurs. His DVD collection was worth thousands and his jokes, even more. Creativity oozes out his pores. You'd give anything to be paired with him in group projects because he could create elaborate theme songs and score As. He was going places, and Hollywood was his first stop.

Pete moved across the country after graduation with dreams of pursuing screenwriting. Five years into working in the entertainment industry, discouragement began to creep in. He was working on set and positioning himself to be a screenwriter. It wasn't looking the way he had dreamed, and he began doubting himself. Rooted in insecurity, he gave up.

He sold his stuff, shipped back his prized collections of dinosaurs and DVDs, and found someone to take his place in his apartment.

The night before his airplane flew home with his dreams, he held a going-away party with his community. There, a friend brought him a gift. He set it in his room for later.

The party ended, and Pete settled into his final night in Hollywood. He went out to run some last-minute errands and ran into a former coworker.

Pete told him he was leaving in the morning.

But his coworker said Pete was meant to be a screenwriter and couldn't give up. He encouraged Pete in his talents and abilities and spoke life into him.

Back at his apartment later that night, Pete was finishing packing and saw the present from his friend. The card held a message similar to the one his former coworker had just spoken to him.

As he opened the gift, he saw two books about screenwriting. He started flipping through the pages and encountered words that fueled his creativity. Pete realized that many professionals shared his worries about a writing career. The words in the books addressed the internal challenges he faced, and he no longer felt alone.

And it changed Pete's story.

People collide at the right moment to encourage a dying passion. They see you, know your potential, and believe in you when you don't. God used community in Pete's life, and it inspired him to fight.

He ended up staying in LA and is now a producer and writer for a prime-time TV show.

I told you he was going places!

Imagine if those two friends hadn't had the guts to encourage Pete's dreams. Or if Pete had remained stuck in insecurity.

Do you see the power of community?

In the book *Whiter Than Snow*, Paul Tripp says, "We weren't created to be independent, autonomous, or self-sufficient. We were made to live in a humble, worshipful, and loving dependency upon God and in a loving and humble interdependency with others. Our lives were designed to be community projects."[1]

You are not meant to do life alone. Get in a group that can get uncomfortable in an effort to grow together. Where laughter happens and tears lead to prayer. Where vulnerability is embraced and pizza is shared. Find fellow creatives who are passionately pursuing their creativity. Talk about your projects; offer resources and wisdom. Make jokes about jump cuts, aspect ratios, and other geeky things. Give each other feedback if asked and hold one another accountable to pursuing new ideas and innovations. Ask hard questions and encourage one another in chasing dreams. This is how greater creativity is unleashed.

Love one another in your God-given uniqueness, celebrate your friends' talents and gifts, and cheer them on as they chase their calling. Get messy in community as you uncover your creativity killers and commit to overcoming them together. Understand the power of encouragement and speak life over one another. You never know when someone is close to giving up on a dream.

Engage in community with creatives where you commiserate in the hard, collaborate when called, and celebrate all Christ is doing. Like the artist splattering color onto a canvas, when you take a step back, you'll see the beauty community has created. Community changed Pete's story, and God can use it to change yours.

TIPS & TRICKS
from an Industry Expert

PETE
television writer and producer

TOP 12 LESSONS FROM A TV SHOW WRITER

1. One of the most important lessons I've learned as a TV writer is that writing is rewriting. Nobody in the history of all of writing has ever written a flawless first draft...of anything.

2. So even if you're happy with your work, that doesn't mean it can't be better.

3. You should sleep on it.

4. Revisit tricky plot points and character dynamics.

5. Explore different storylines for a day or two.

6. Button up all the logic.

7. Do more research.

8. Try to beat every line of dialogue with a better line of dialogue.

9. Read it out loud to yourself.

10. Don't be afraid to give it to friends or fellow writers for notes...and try not to get defensive when they have criticism. Hear them out—they are your audience. You're too close to your own work to know how good it is. Outsiders have a unique perspective and can help you gauge whether your writing makes any sense.

11. Battle testing your drafts will better prepare you for the piles of notes you're inevitably going to get anyway. Whether it's the studio, the network, a director, or an actor requesting changes, you will have to make changes along the road. The more you've driven through every story and character avenue, the more of an expert mechanic you'll be when it's time to do a tune-up.

12. So the next time you think you've put that cherry on top of that writing sundae, listen to that inner voice. The one that is tapping you on the shoulder and telling you that you can do better. That something isn't quite working yet—that writing is rewriting.

CREATIVE PROCESS

REWRITE

Writing is rewriting. Since you already slept on it, make yesterday's work better. Ask a friend or fellow creative ninja for feedback on what you wrote in the previous challenge. Write down their suggestions.

DREAM BIGGER.

23

Allow Yourself to Dream

Miracles start to happen when you give as much energy to your dreams as you do to your fears.

RICHARD WILKINS

What do a policeman, astronaut, rock star, and author all have in common?

Ding, ding, ding! They all have dream jobs.[1]

> As a child, when you were asked, "What do you want to be when you grow up?" how did you respond?

_____

_____

_____

_____

Did your dreams develop as you grew, or has fear stopped you? Could it be that dreams are lost when people realize they have to be fully functioning humans in a society that obsesses over money? Along the way, the genius-level creatives and imaginative children grew up. We often trade our dreams and abilities for comfortability and security.

Does the responsibility of "adulting" mean we have to put our passions on the back burner? No, it means we have to fight to pursue hard things! God has entrusted you with gifts and talents that you now get to steward well. When you allow yourself to dream about your jobs, ideas, projects, and passions, you can unleash a greater creative freedom.

LET GO OF THE LABELS THAT LIMIT YOUR ABILITY TO DREAM AND LISTEN AS GOD DEFINES YOUR DESTINY.

Dreams shift and change with the seasons. When I worked in ministry and also as a freelance video editor, I began evaluating the dreams God had placed on my heart. I felt called to be a speaker. I wasn't even sure what being a speaker meant, but I knew God could speak through a donkey, so I was 80 percent sure I would qualify for the job.[2]

I told one person my dream, and he said, "Why would you do that?" With one innocent question, I tucked that dream away and vowed to never talk about it again. Because *why would I do that?*

Years went by, and as with any dream, it never went away. It lurked in my mind and tugged on my soul, silently waiting for me to take action. I played hard to get with that dream for ten years because people pleasing, insecurity, and fear were killing my creativity. I prayed and prayed and finally mustered the courage to throw up my hands in surrender—I told God I'd do it. Then I sat and I waited...and waited...and cried...and waited. If I got the memo, why didn't anyone else? In my romanticized view, when I finally said yes, God would magically tell church leaders and pastors that I was called to speaking.

Believe it or not, it didn't happen that way. I had to actually *do* something.

As I began to position myself to chase this dream, I ended up at a conference for speakers and writers. One session during worship, I cried the whole time. (Sometimes chasing scary things requires tears.) I was crying because it all felt so big and overwhelming. This God-sized dream was weighing me down, and it seemed like too much.

Have you ever felt this way?

My tears during worship released some of my anxiety, but I still wasn't trusting God. The dream felt so big, and I was questioning whether I was qualified.

I ugly cried my way into a beautiful prayer room that the conference facilitators had prepared for moments like this. As I sat tucked away in the corner, listening to music and praying, I had an encounter with God. It was as if I were having a daydream. I saw blackness everywhere. Then I saw a giant dome surround the darkness. In the giant dome was a teeny-tiny dot. The huge dome represented my dream of public speaking. The little dot represented me.

I felt as if Holy Spirit said, **"Do you trust Me to fill the space between you and your dream?"** You know when He asks a question, it's not because He doesn't know the answer.

Of course, I replied in my heart. Then God began to fill the space between myself and my dream. Before I knew it, the dark space was lit and was spilling over beyond the dome of my dream. Then Holy Spirit told me to dream bigger.

Holy Spirit showed me that He'd fill the space between me and my God-given goals and dreams; all I had to do was be obedient.

The same thing applies to all of us.

God fills the space with people, resources, tools, trainings, love, and encouragement. He fills it with ideas, songs, movies, art.

Look at the story of stuttering Moses in the Bible. God gave Moses the gift of Aaron, who often acted as his spokesman. God filled the space for Moses. God will equip you in ways applicable to your calling. It reminds me of that saying,

GOD DOESN'T CALL THE QUALIFIED, HE QUALIFIES THE CALLED.

"Obey Me, and I will be your God and you will be my people. Walk in obedience to all I command you, that it may go well with you."

JEREMIAH 7:23

It's time to chase those dreams that are locked up or forgotten. Maybe you're an accountant with a dream to be an artist. May that God-sized dream be fueled by divine creativity.

Maybe as a little boy, you had a love for airplanes, but as you grew, it got overshadowed by the need for security. May that dream to study aviation take flight.

Perhaps you're facing insecurity but feel called to produce a show. My prayer is that you will walk in obedience and trust God to fill the spaces.

SIMPLE PRAYER
Lord, may we become dreamers and doers who chase after You. Amen!

DAY 23
Creative Challenge

PHOTOGRAPHY
CAPTURE EMOTION

To create a powerful emotion, you need genuine interaction and connection. Take a photo of someone or something, from a playful puppy to a pensive person. Make it your goal to capture a powerful emotion or expression through the lens. Then ask your friends if they can guess what emotion you captured. Tap into your previous photography lessons about composition and lighting.

THE GREATER THE HUMILITY, THE
GREATER THE OPPORTUNITY
FOR CREATIVITY.

Tolerate Failure

The only man who never makes a mistake
is the man who never does anything.

THEODORE ROOSEVELT

A bad review of your film, the boss's hatred of your pitch idea, or your loss of the role in the play you wanted can be seen as a failure. We've all had a creative failure, faced bitter rejection, or received harsh criticism. **As God-fearing creatives, we need a faith that's bigger than our failures and rejections.** That faith will lead to greater humility, and the greater the humility, the greater the opportunity for creativity.

After graduating college, my friends and I moved to Hollywood, eager to start our careers in the entertainment industry. We were desperate to land a gig somewhere on set with a studio or, for me, in a postproduction facility. I saw a job listing at a post house and decided to apply. They listed a fax number but no company name. I investigated my way into their hearts as I figured out the business name and made reference to it many times in my cover letter. The ninja skills landed me my first job in Hollywood...as a receptionist.

It was the typical entry-level gig that consisted of getting coffee, managing spreadsheets, and answering phones—which my friends loved, because they prank called me multiple times a day. The job did have lots of perks, like free daily lunch and a glimpse into the process of editing everything from TV shows to concerts. My favorite perk was that my boss let me use the editing equipment after hours so I could teach myself industry-standard software. One night I stayed late editing, and around ten, the sound guy, Kevin, frantically came looking for me.

"Jenny, we really need your help! There are two executives in the sound studio, and we need someone to record a voiceover. Can you do it?"

At that point in my career, I did whatever was asked in an attempt to figure out where I fit in. This was a big step up from being a coffee getter, and it could have been a big break into launching a voiceover career I didn't even know I wanted. I said okay and followed him to his booth.

A promo spot for a movie was due to the studio the next day, but for some reason, the picture was out of sync with the actress's voice. Since I was the only female left in the building...I got the gig.

IT'S NOT THAT THEY SAW POTENTIAL IN ME. THEY WERE JUST DESPERATE.

The recording booth had foam pads on the wall to help with the acoustics. A fancy microphone was in the middle of the room with a stand to hold papers. Kevin opened the door and showed me where to stand and what to read. Then he went into an adjacent room with his sound board, HDTV, and the studio execs. Between us was a giant glass window where they could watch my performance.

Kevin came over the room speakers, also known as "the God mic," and said, "Jenny, it's less than ten words. You'll do great! Oh, and you have to do it in a British accent."

British accent? I started panicking. *I can barely speak English, and this guy wants me to do it in a British accent?* I felt terrified but didn't want to let my insecurity determine my decisions, so I cleared my voice and got ready.

"Rolling!" he yelled as he over-accentuated his finger point at me through the glass.

The trailer started to play, and I channeled my inner Kate Winslet. "Would YOU LIGHT *me* a candle on MY BIRTHHHHHHHHDAY?"

I sounded more like a squeaky Bart Simpson who'd had four cups of coffee and then was mauled by bears.

The studio execs were squirming in their seats, and I could feel their criticism. We all knew it wasn't pretty. Kevin came over the God mic and tried to coach me.

"Tone it down a bit, punch that line here, go slower…Take 2. Action!"

"WOULD yooooooooou light me a candle ON MY birthday?"

Now I sounded like a drunk dinosaur. I'm not sure what they sound like, but I'm pretty sure my voiceover was an accurate representation.

They were desperate, but I was wasting an hour of everybody's time trying to deliver an Emmy-worthy moment…a moment that didn't exist within my realm of talents.

After every take, I could see the studio execs' disappointed glances at each other. I was horrible and wasn't getting any better.

I failed. I had miscalculated my abilities, and my voiceover career was fading to black before it even began.

There were two ways I could greet this failure: (1) I could dwell on it, let it define me, and give up, or (2) I could figure out how to be forward-thinking in my failure and find a way around it.

Then into the fancy mic, I stopped attempting voiceovers about birthdays and offered a real solution. "Why don't we call my friend who's just down the road? She lives five minutes away and will be able to deliver this line."

Without hesitation, the studio execs said yes. I'm also pretty sure all the angels rejoiced because they no longer had to listen to my Bart Simpson bear attack–drunk dino voiceover. The execs' lack of hesitation was a shot to my ego, but Jesus loved me nonetheless.

I called my friend Erin Brett, who arrived in minutes. Sitting on the other side of the glass with the sound mixer and studio execs, I felt secure—secure in the fact that my failure didn't define me.

Erin delivered the line in one take, and we all got to go home. She has since been dubbed "One-Take Wonder."

My friend Anne B. Say believes our past experiences should be "redeemed and upgraded." My voiceover failure has been redeemed multiple times as I've coached and trained others from the other side of the glass. As a video editor, I've been able to utilize my experience of failing to help guide others who record voiceovers for the pieces I edit.

THOUGHTS ON FAILURE

- If you're never failing, you aren't taking enough creative risks.
- We can grow from our mistakes by looking forward and trusting God to equip us.
- Failing can lead to beautiful breakthroughs.
- Defeat comes when your value is determined by your critics and not by Christ.
- Tolerating creative failure produces humility.

What was your last failure?

_____

_____

_____

_____

In what ways did it leave you feeling humbled?

_____

_____

When you create from a humble space, you're willing to go into uncomfortable, awkward, and creatively risky situations. Those situations may produce fun opportunities with big results. Humility is the key to tolerate failure, rejection, and criticism. It reminds us that we are human, teaches us how to grow, and reminds us on whom to place our focus (Jesus). **"Humble yourselves, therefore, under God's mighty hand, that he may lift you up in due time."**[2]

SIMPLE PRAYER

Lord, when we face creative failure, criticism, or rejection, help us
to rely on Holy Spirit for wisdom, strength, and security. Amen.

TIPS & TRICKS
from an Industry Expert

ERIN BRETT
Hollywood marketing producer and writer

"Constructive criticism." It's a phrase that's made you cringe since childhood, right? But I'm here to plead in its defense. Constructive criticism can have a healthy place in the creative environment. Navigating criticism can be difficult, but it's a process that gets easier with time and practice.

Art can be subjective. What soars for one person might sink for another. And while some creative projects are intended for private reflection and enjoyment, others are meant to be consumed and shared.

"Creative types" shouldn't exist inside a bubble. Creative growth comes from moving outside our comfort zone and embracing new ideas. Sometimes, this type of growth can sting—especially when it comes in the form of constructive criticism.

I get it. No one likes to have his or her work judged, and art can bring out our most sensitive and protective feelings. I've certainly had days where creative notes have made me cry. Art is personal. It's not just numbers on a spreadsheet.

But by opening yourself up to constructive criticism, you can enter into a world of possibilities. It won't always be easy. And it won't always be what you want to hear. But sometimes it can spark an idea that can take your work to the next level.

My advice: start small. Show some of your projects to friends you trust. Ask them what they like and what they'd change. Ask for *specifics* (this is key!). Do they like the color of the background? Might another piece of music work better? Give yourself time to reflect on their suggestions and consider them sincerely. Resist the urge to be defensive (this is the hardest part!). Remember that they are not attacking your work, but helping you look at things from another perspective. Give some of their suggestions a try. If they don't work, you can always go back to your original work.

But in my experience, this will actually spark a brand-new idea. And your art will be better for it.

DAY 24
Creative Challenge

PERFORMANCE

VOICEOVER

Congrats! A client just booked you for a voiceover for a 30-second movie trailer! It's a quirky comedy called *Creativity Camp*. Speak clearly and confidently, and work on the spacing between words.

Oh, and the client requested two versions: one utilizing your normal voice and one with a British accent. (You're welcome.) Have fun! Grab your phone or fancy mic, channel your inner radio voice, and record the lines below:

Creativity Camp

30-SECOND SPOT

In a world where creativity is fading and life is boring,
a group of misfits set out to find themselves and their paintbrushes.
This summer, experience a story of discovery and collaboration at *Creativity Camp*,
where it's great to create.

Rated PG.

IN MY CREATIVITY, I WILL CHALLENGE,
STRETCH, AND PUSH PAST MY
COMFORT ZONES. AND WHEN
I FAIL, I WON'T FEEL ALONE. FOR
MY IDENTITY IS ROOTED IN CHRIST,
WHO AWAKENS MY SOUL.

Identity in Christ

Number one, put God first in everything you do.
Everything that you think you see in me and
everything you think I've accomplished and
everything you think I have...everything I have
is by the grace of God, understand that.
It's a gift.

DENZEL WASHINGTON

Whether we realize it or not, labels create our identity. Labels can come from ourselves, the world, or God. They shape our purpose and destiny. Sometimes they point to something big, sometimes to something little. The labels that stick can limit what we allow ourselves to become, or they can push us on to greater things!

Whom or what are you letting define you?

_____

_____

_____

_____

"Let your roots grow down into him, and let your lives be built on him. Then your faith will grow strong in the truth you were taught, and you will overflow with thankfulness."[1]

When you know God, you'll know what's *not* God. You have to fight to establish healthy identity. You can be a Christian but lose sight of Christ. Become self-aware through prayer and ask God what labels are sticking to you. Examine yourself and learn to walk in wholeness and purpose. Rip off those hurtful labels and stick God's thoughts all over yourself instead.

MY IDENTITY IS NOT

my sin,

struggles,

poor health,

rejections from friends,

or limitations.

MY IDENTITY IS NOT

my job,

stuff I make,

achievements,

fancy clothes,

or low blows.

MY IDENTITY IS MY SAVIOR.

I am a child of God, a friend of Jesus, a whole new person, a temple where Holy Spirit lives, and God's masterpiece. I am wonderfully created in God's likeness, totally and completely forgiven, and spiritually alive. I am the salt of the earth and the light of the world. I am part of a chosen generation, an overcomer, and a conqueror. I am bold, not fearful, and I carry peace. I am never alone, and I matter. I am greatly loved.

> "The world is unprincipled. It's dog-eat-dog out there! The world doesn't fight fair. But we don't live or fight our battles that way—never have and never will. The tools of our trade aren't for marketing or manipulation, but they are for demolishing that entire massively corrupt culture. We use our powerful God-tools for smashing warped philosophies, tearing down barriers erected against the truth of God, fitting every loose thought and emotion and impulse into the structure of life shaped by Christ. Our tools are ready at hand for clearing the ground of every obstruction and building lives of obedience into maturity."
>
> 2 Corinthians 10:3-6 MSG

Peter denied Jesus three times but later loyally proclaimed the Gospel and became known as a pillar of the early church. Imagine if the label "unloyal" had stuck to him.

Paul was responsible for the deaths of many early Christians but later became a missionary, apostle, and writer of the early church. Imagine if the label "murderer" had stuck to him.

Shift your perspective off of what you were and onto who God says you are.

Are you ready to start "tearing down barriers erected against the truth of God"? Preserve your new identity. Read verses in the Bible that relate to your healthy labels and speak them over yourself. We have the power to go into battle with the full armor of God. So pick up that sword and meditate on the Word daily. **Healthy identity produces a security that fosters greater creativity.** Placing your identity in our Savior will give you the confidence to try new things, pursue big ideas, and trust Him above all things.

DAY 25
Creative Challenge

PHOTOGRAPHY

IDENTITY

In photography, negative space in a photo is the space that surrounds the point of interest. Often, negative space has minimal details. When used properly, it can create a mood and give the interest point room to breathe.

Pray and meditate on the word **identity**. Take a photo that represents that word artistically. Challenge yourself to use negative space in the shot.

After you've captured just the right image, check off this challenge on the contents page.

CREATE FROM A SPACE OF SELF-REFLECTION AND GRACE.

Vulnerability

He said to me, "My grace is sufficient for you,
for my power is made perfect in weakness."
Therefore I will boast all the more gladly about my
weaknesses, so that Christ's power may rest on me.

2 CORINTHIANS 12:9

I didn't recognize the person's name in my inbox. Unsure if I was opening up spam or a Nigerian email scam, I began to read the email anyway. Halfway through, I ugly cried. I'm talking Hallmark movie marathon ugly cried. The words I was reading came from a woman who was navigating a vulnerable situation similar to one I had written about.

Months earlier, I felt as if I was supposed to spill my guts on a very scandalous subject—abuse in the church. I did *not* want to write a blog series on this because that meant I had to actually...write.

Write *and* share intimate details from my own story? No, thanks!

I'm all for vulnerability...as long as my involvement is cheering on other dudes and dudettes from the sidelines. I mean, who really wants to plaster the internet with personal church wounds and other hot messes?

Am I right?

Life isn't always unicorns, confetti, and cupcakes. When the party stops and you're face-to-face with heartache, failure, or hard circumstances, how do you process that? Do you close your eyes and pretend it isn't there?

I get it, because I was once that person.

Or do you wrestle through your own story with the Ultimate Creator, willing to get a little messy as you navigate the ups and downs of life?

As creatives, we can pursue opportunities to tell our story through art, song writing, painting, design, videos, or other new and innovative ways. We need to give ourselves the freedom to create from a space of self-reflection and grace.

WHEN WE COMMUNICATE OUR WEAKNESS, WE CREATE AN OPPORTUNITY FOR OTHERS TO CONNECT TO GOD'S STRENGTH.

This whole "be creatively vulnerable" thing is about demonstrating our humanity and imperfection. We're communicating a deeper need for the One who is perfect. When we set aside time to tell our story in a creative way, we open up space for raw vulnerability based on the perfect saving grace of Jesus. I'm not perfect, but I know the One who is.

You aren't called to be a tortured artist. **You are called to express the heart of the Ultimate Creator.**

So what does that look like for you?

For me, it was taking a step of faith and diving into a topic that had been forgiven and forgotten for more than ten years. With my best friends and husband and through prayer, I spent time processing whether I should actually write the blog series. I gradually realized that staying silent was no longer an option for me, so I got uncomfortable and wrote.

I knew God wanted to bring others freedom, and I trusted Him to use my vulnerability to do just that. I'm the girl who would publish a blog post—and then turn off the computer just to keep myself from deleting it. So I'm speaking from experience when I say that baring your soul can stir up insecurities or a fear of rejection from those you are being vulnerable with. Thank God for God, because He's bigger than all of that! Holy artistic expression releases a power that is bigger than any fear or insecurity. It helps you to place your trust in God and know that He's going to finish writing the story.

It's not really about you anyway—it's about Him.

Creating from this space can be difficult, uncomfortable, and exhausting. What you create can be an outward expression of your pain, and God can use the process to bring you greater healing and freedom. When we share our broken heart through art in a healthy way, we allow God to breathe new life into painful circumstances.

Redemptive vulnerability means letting God exchange your pain for His promises. He works *all things* together for the good of those who love Him.[1] Understanding this promise produces new life in you and your community.

But what does that look like?

It might look like letting God turn our bad situations into something good. That creative process is often a struggle, but it brings freedom to those who connect with our work and our Savior.

Throughout the process of sharing my story, I experienced many moments of self-reflection and asking God, "What if?" and "Who am I?" A bigger picture of God's grace and goodness gradually emerged.

And now, reading this email from a stranger more than a decade later, I could see that picture more clearly. As I sat there in a puddle of tears, I knew going to that creative space was worth all my effort and discomfort. This woman had a similar story and was struggling through her own church wounds. She revealed what she was wrestling through, thanked me, and closed her email with this: "I wanted to tell you that you helped me be brave."

That is why we create.

So if you are fighting a battle, carrying deep sorrow, or reflecting on a life-transforming experience, grab that pen, paintbrush, or guitar and let it out. You aren't just communicating your story; you're communicating God's story. His power, grace, and goodness will shine in what you do. So search for God in the raw moments of discomfort and invite Him into your process. Holy Spirit might inspire you to create one of the most beautiful reflections of your heart.

Our world needs you to embrace vulnerability in a redemptive way because your story—God's story—carries the power to make a difference.

SIMPLE PRAYER

God, we trust You to write our story. Amen!

DAY 26
Creative Challenge

WRITING
YOUR STORY / GOD'S STORY

Fill in the blanks below, and don't forget to invite Holy Spirit into your process.

I was _____

I am _____

"If anyone is in Christ, the new creation has come: The old has gone, the new is here!"

2 CORINTHIANS 5:17

"I PRAY THAT GOD,
THE SOURCE OF HOPE,
WILL FILL YOU COMPLETELY
WITH JOY AND PEACE BECAUSE
YOU TRUST IN HIM.
THEN YOU WILL OVERFLOW
WITH CONFIDENT HOPE
THROUGH THE POWER
OF THE HOLY SPIRIT."
ROMANS 15:13 NLT

Invite Holy Spirit

Without the Spirit of God, we can do nothing. We are as ships without wind or chariots without steeds. Like branches without sap, we are withered. Like coals without fire, we are useless. As an offering without the sacrificial flame, we are unaccepted.

CHARLES SPURGEON

Have you ever felt stuck on a creative project? At a loss for inspiration, with your project seeming dull and lifeless? Sometimes I struggle with feeling creatively depleted. One of my jobs is an art director for a Christian publishing company. We give our clients three cover concepts, and they get to pick their favorite. The other day, I was working on creating cover art for a book titled *Beyond Hope?*

Ironically enough, I was feeling beyond hope myself. I was five hours in, and nothing in my designs was making sense. My husband was watching the kids, and I was locked away in my office trying to make something work. It was as if I couldn't budge the door of creativity open. I tried to muster up my creativity by turning on music. When that didn't work, I tried turning it off. I did some stretches, drank more coffee, and even changed my scenery, looking for inspiration. Then I took a nap because I work from home and was feeling bored with myself.

After I woke up, I sat at the computer and realized I hadn't invited Holy Spirit into my creative process. As a result, I had wasted five hours.

BEING FUELED BY SELF
COMPROMISES OUR CREATIVE INTEGRITY.
BEING FUELED BY HOLY SPIRIT
PRODUCES DIVINE CREATIVITY.

Holy Spirit resides in the hearts of God's people.[1] He produces in us the fruit of the Spirit as He guides, directs, comforts, and influences us.[2] The apostle Paul reveals how this worked in his preaching: "Rather than using clever and persuasive speeches, I relied only on the power of the Holy Spirit. I did this so you would trust not in human wisdom but in the power of God."[3] We can look to Paul as an example of trusting the power of Holy Spirit to bring wisdom so we can effectively communicate the message God has placed on our heart.

Holy Spirit can bring creative confidence and innovative thoughts to us. As I sat at my desk, I repented for not including God in my creative design process. Sitting still, I waited and trusted Holy Spirit to speak. I love the way Bob Briner talks about this in his book *Roaring Lambs*: "Christians with direct access to the Creator of the universe and with the indwelling of the Holy Spirit should be and could be the most brilliantly dazzling artists imaginable."[4]

As I settled into my prayer, shifting my focus and inviting Holy Spirit's wisdom, a photo came to the forefront of my mind that I had passed by earlier as I was digging through stock images. It was of two trees. One tree was actually nothing more than a dead stump. Was it beyond hope? Next to that tree was another that was firmly planted, alive, and flourishing. I found the stock image and spent 30 minutes turning that thought into artwork. It was a cover that conveyed the promise of new life. The clients connected with that cover art and used it on their book. *Thank You, God!*

God holds the key to unlock new possibility—all we have to do is ask. When you invite Holy Spirit into your creative process, you're asking for new inspiration and ideas to reflect God's creative heart. You are seeking Holy Spirit to define your purpose for each piece, speech, or creative endeavor. Be in His presence through worship, the Word, and prayer.

While promoting *The Passion of the Christ*, Mel Gibson said, "I'm not a preacher and I'm not a pastor, but I really feel my career was leading me to make this. The Holy Ghost was working through me on this film, and I was just directing traffic."[5] He was trusting the power of Holy Spirit to help him effectively communicate through film.

Are you trusting Holy Spirit to inspire your creativity and to work through you? He can use your creations to help others connect to Him. That is why people tend to gravitate toward innovations and thoughts that are divinely inspired. Collaborating with God brings us into the wholeness of who we were designed to be. So, dazzling artist, let Holy Spirit fuel your creativity.

SIMPLE PRAYER
Lord, teach us to understand Holy Spirit's voice in our lives! Amen.

DIGITAL STORY

ACTS

You are making a movie based on the New Testament book of Acts. Come up with a clever movie title and write it down. By utilizing an app on your smartphone, graphic design software, or that trusty pencil, design a movie poster.

MAINTAIN YOUR RELATIONSHIP WITH
CHRIST BY REMAINING
SURRENDERED IN YOUR LIFE.

28 Total Surrender

*Come, let us bow down in worship,
let us kneel before the LORD our Maker.*

PSALM 95:6

*Lift up your hands to the holy place
and give thanks to the Lord.*

PSALM 134:2 NLV

"Stick 'em up!"

Have you ever seen a movie where someone gets robbed by gunpoint? The victim typically hands over his stuff and raises his hands to show he isn't in control. This is the posture of surrender.

Here's the difference between surrendering at gunpoint and surrendering to God: Living a life of surrender isn't giving up; it's looking up.

I heard a pastor say he literally started his day on his knees. Before his feet touched the ground, he rolled out of bed into a posture of surrender. Inspired by his example, I did the same thing for months. I rolled out of my bed and fell on my knees, surrendering my day to God. It seems I was more clumsy than the pastor, because I often got wrapped up in my blankets, awkwardly laughing on the way down. The physical action of kneeling or lifting our hands is a way to connect with God in reverent submission to His will. By consistently surrendering my day to Jesus, I developed and maintained a Kingdom mindset. I became more self-aware and more focused on glorifying God in my projects and interactions, and my relationship with Jesus grew stronger.

How can you position yourself to surrender your day-to-day life to God? Let's look to Jesus as the ultimate example of self-surrender. The night before He was killed on the cross, Jesus "fell to the ground and prayed for a way out: 'Papa, Father, you can—can't you?—get me out of this. Take this cup away from me. But please, not what I want—what do *you* want?'"[1] As He contemplated His pending death, Jesus surrendered His will to the Father.

When you're living a life of total surrender, you have to choose to be obedient to God's will rather than your own human desires and wants. One celeb is attempting just that...I'm a Belieber.

No, that's not a typo. I have a love for Justin Bieber. He's one of the biggest performers on the planet and has sometimes used his platform to share his faith. In an interview with *Complex*

Magazine, Justin said, "Sometimes when I don't feel like doing something, but I know it's right, I remember, *I'm pretty sure Jesus didn't feel like going to the cross and dying.*"[2]

That's surrender. Putting God's agenda above your own. As a result, Bieber has been using his influence to share the Gospel. During a sold-out show in Sydney in March 2017, Justin appeared on the stage in a transparent box with the handwritten words: "Mark my words, Jesus loves you!!!!"[3]

You surrender by trusting that your creative flow comes from the Ultimate Creator. You let His plans override yours. You submit your art, ideas, thoughts, and dreams to the Father and ask, "What do You want?" As you put your hands up in surrender to God, you yield to His will for your life and trust Him with the bigger picture. In *My Utmost for His Highest,* Oswald Chambers writes, "The most important aspect of Christianity is not the work we do but the relationship we maintain and the surrounding influence and qualities produced by that relationship. That is all God asks us to give our attention to, and it is the one thing that is continually under attack."[5]

Maintain your relationship with Christ by remaining surrendered in your life.

SIMPLE PRAYER

Lord, help us have a posture of surrender in our
daily living and while we create. Amen.

ART

SKETCH

Sketch an object that is right in front of you. *You've got this!*

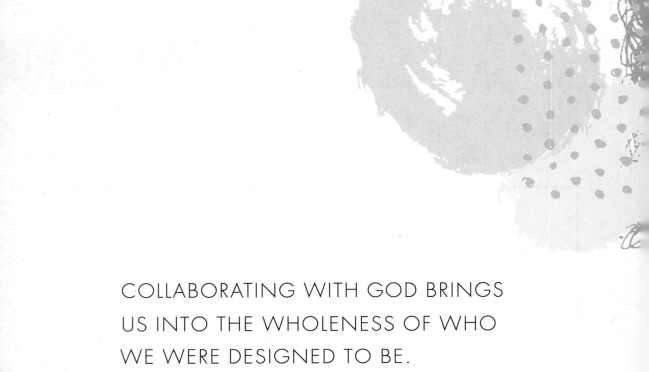

COLLABORATING WITH GOD BRINGS
US INTO THE WHOLENESS OF WHO
WE WERE DESIGNED TO BE.

You Are Chosen

We are united in purpose but unique in calling.

BRAYDEN BROOKSHIER

Today we're going to talk about the dudes God chose to build the tabernacle. If you were the kid who did all the extracurricular activities in school, then read through Exodus chapters 25–30 first. You'll get a materials list, ideas for fashion, and math things that I struggle to wrap my head around. God gave some pretty detailed measurements and directions. He's way better than IKEA. I'm dying to know if you can read through that without coveting those goat-haired curtains.[1] Who knew the Bible could be so hipster chic?

> "Then the LORD said to Moses, 'See, I have chosen Bezalel son of Uri, the son of Hur, of the tribe of Judah, and I have filled him with the Spirit of God, with wisdom, with understanding, with knowledge and with all kinds of skills—to make artistic designs for work in gold, silver and bronze, to cut and set stones, to work in wood, and to engage in all kinds of crafts. Moreover, I have appointed Oholiab son of Ahisamak, of the tribe of Dan, to help him. Also I have given ability to all the skilled workers to make everything I have commanded you.'"
>
> EXODUS 31:1-6

Okay, let's talk about Bezalel. He was the chief artisan on the project—basically the Spielberg of making *stuff*. God specifically chose Bezalel for a specific task...and God chose you!

You are chosen. In this season, you may be chosen to raise your littles, write a film, make jewelry, or take photos in Africa. As a believer (not Belieber, like in yesterday's devotion), you are chosen. Depending on your season of life, your chosen tasks may change, but you'll always be chosen to be a child of God.[2]

God chose Bezalel to make artistic designs and then equipped him with Holy Spirit. We, too, can have supernatural superpowers to help us do what God wants done. Holy Spirit will bring you wisdom, understanding, knowledge, and even skill as you step into the creative tasks God is calling you to.

He'll even bring you a crew!

Remember in Day 23, I described a magical Jesus moment I had when God showed me He'd bring me people, tools, and resources to help fulfill what I felt called to do? What's going down with the tabernacle crew is an amazing example of this. As you read Exodus 31:6, you can see how God appointed talented people to assist Bezalel as he worked on this project. Not only that, but God gave His workers the ability and skill to make everything He commanded. They were Spirit-filled servants who helped to build the Kingdom.

Let this passage be an encouragement to you as you step into your calling.

YOU ARE CHOSEN.

Minister and author John Piper says, "The more we consider being chosen, the more the wonder of it grows."[3] Consider being chosen. Trust Holy Spirit to anoint your work and tasks, whether you're a teacher, crafter, coach, or singer. You are chosen to serve others in a way that brings God glory!

Spend time in prayer. How are you chosen?

_____

_____

_____

_____

SIMPLE PRAYER

Lord, show us what tasks You have chosen for us. May You
bring them to the forefront of our minds. Fill us with Holy Spirit
so we can achieve all You've set before us. Amen!

CREATIVE PROCESS

UNIQUE TASKS

Think outside the box and come up with as many uses as possible for the items listed below. For example, a glass could hold soda or become a vase for flowers. God has chosen many tasks for you too!

CHAIR	BOOK	YOU

Thoughts or Reflections

Get Social

Imagine me throwing confetti at your face. Woohoo—you made it through act 3! Tomorrow, we'll have a wrap party for our last lesson, so don't ditch out.

LET'S RECAP SOME KEY TAKEAWAYS

- Unleash your creativity by developing healthy creative habits, mindsets, and obedience.
- Creativity is like a muscle; it must be challenged, stretched, and pushed past its comfort zone.
- You are a proven miracle and unique masterpiece.
- Engage in community with creatives where you commiserate in the hard, collaborate when called, and celebrate all Christ is doing.
- Let go of the labels that limit your ability to dream, and listen as God defines your destiny.
- Healthy identity produces a security that fosters greater creativity.
- The creative process is often a struggle, but the freedom it brings to those who connect with our work and our Savior is worth the effort.
- Collaborating with God brings us into the wholeness of who we were designed to be.
- Being fueled by self compromises our creative integrity. Being fueled by Holy Spirit produces divine creativity.
- Maintain your relationship with Christ by remaining surrendered in your life.

YOU ARE CHOSEN.

FREESTYLE

GET SOCIAL

Unleash your creativity on a friend or family member. Remember how we learned about the power of community? Pray and ask Holy Spirit whom you can encourage in his or her dreams today. Jot down that name and some thoughts. Reach out with a handwritten note or a special drawing, or create a graphic design with an inspirational Bible verse.

THE *STUFF* YOU CREATE HOLDS POWER.

That's a Wrap

A friend of mine was enduring a horrendous time in her life. She had a lot of "church wounds" from her childhood and wasn't interested in getting to know Jesus. Before meeting up with her one day, I was praying and felt led to give her one of the books I designed.

Later that day, I gave her the book. Since she knows what I do, she asked if it was about Jesus. I told her it was.

She told me she wouldn't read the book, but as she glanced at it, she noticed the cover. The cover art shows a man hanging from a cliff. It instantly reminded her of a sermon she heard growing up. The simple cover I had created opened up a great conversation. She was reminded that God is there—all she had to do was put her trust in Him.

I tell you that story to reiterate this...

The *stuff* you create holds power. Power to open up conversations, influence culture, and change the nation. I believe it because I've seen it. Look at *Hacksaw Ridge*, a film and true story of faith in action.

Look at the creatives who influence others. Like Korn's Brian "Head" Welch, who prays with concertgoers outside his concerts. Or C.S. Lewis. As a child, he was enchanted by fantastic animals and tales of gallantry in imaginative lands.[1] He went on to create The Chronicles of Narnia, a series set in a fantasy world with mythical beasts and talking animals, written with Christian themes.

Then we have you, creative ninja. **You were created to create!** You're fueled by Holy Spirit, which means you are chock-full of divine creativity. He's equipping you with the skills and resources to make *stuff* that will change your world and bring glory to His.

HE'S BRINGING FREEDOM TO YOU.
HE'S EMPOWERING YOU.
HE'S INSPIRING YOU.
AND HE'S CALLING YOU.

Are you ready to pursue those creative dreams? You aren't just empowered for this. **You were made for this. You are created to cocreate so that others will desire to connect with and reflect the Ultimate Creator.**

HAPPY CREATING!

WRITING
FIRST AND LAST

Write the first sentence and the last sentence of Jesus's memoir.

Congratulations!
You finished all 31 challenges.

Notes

What Is Courageous Creative?

1. Caroline Leaf, "FINALLY! The Online 21-Day Brain Detox Is Here!!" *Dr. Leaf's Blog,* April 11, 2013, http://drleaf.com/blog/finally-the-online-21-day-brain-detox-is-here/.

1: Creative Assessment

1. Adobe, "State of Create Study: Global benchmark study on attitudes and beliefs about creativity at work, school and home," April 1, 2012, https://www.adobe.com/aboutadobe/pressroom/pdfs/Adobe_State_of_Create_Global_Benchmark_Study.pdf.

2. Bob Blaisdell, ed., *Thoreau: A Book of Quotations* (Mineola, NY: Dover Publications, Inc, 2000), 26.

2: Awe-Inspiring Creator

1. See for example Revelation 21:1-10.

2. Kenneth Mathews, *Genesis 1–11:26,* vol. 1A of *The New American Commentary* (Nashville, TN: Broadman & Holman, 1996), 128.

3. And read Psalm 19:1-4.

3: Relationship

1. John 17:1-5.

2. 2 Corinthians 5:17.

3. Mark 4:35-41.

4: Created to Create

1. Psalm 139:13-18.

2. Ginger Allen, "From Dust to Dust," *Answers in Genesis,* February 15, 2012, https://answersingenesis.org/human-body/from-dust-to-dust/.

3. George Land and Beth Jarman, *Breakpoint and Beyond: Mastering the Future Today* (Scottsdale, AZ: Leadership 2000, 1998), n.p.

5: Creative Assignment

1. Genesis 2:19-20.

2. Ellen Lutwak, "2 Simple Rules for Naming a Successful Product," *Time,* October 17, 2014, http://time.com/3517142/rules-naming-product/.

3. Just as He named other things He created (Genesis 1:5,8,10).

4. Matthew 18:12-14; Luke 15:11-32.

5. Genesis 6:9-22.

6. 1 Kings 3:16-28.

6: Designed with Purpose

Epigraph: Francis Chan, *Crazy Love* (Colorado Springs, CO: David C. Cook, 2013), 47.

1. Westminster Shorter Catechism, *Center for Reformed Theology and Apologetics,* http://www.reformed.org/documents/wsc/.

2. Cited in David C. Cooper, *Repurposing Your Life: Living with Integrity and Passion* (Cleveland, TN: Pathway Press, 2004), 133.

3. Psalm 118:1.

7: Influence Culture

1. Cindy Jacobs, "The Seven Mountains of Societal Influence," *Generals International,* October 20, 2014, https://www.generals.org/rpn/the-seven-mountains/.

2. Matthew 5:16.

3. Whitney Hopler, "Use Your Creativity to Change the Culture," *Crosswalk.com,* January 22, 2012, https://www.crosswalk.com/faith/spiritual-life/use-your-creativity-to-change-the-culture-11573937.html.

10: Fear

Epigraph: John Bevere, *The Fear of the Lord* (Lake Mary, FL: Charisma House, 1997), 3.

1. Proverbs 1:7.

2. Douglas Raine, "The Fear of the Lord," *Full Gospel Businessmen's Training,* http://www.fgbt.org/Lessons/christianity-the-fear-of-the-lord.html.

3. Philippians 2:12.

11: Rules and Regulations

Epigraph: K. Ferlic, "Understanding Play and Its Relation to Creativity," *Releasing Your Unlimited Creativity,* 2006, http://ryuc.info/common/play/understanding_play.htm.

1. Cited in Amy Novotney, "The Science of Creativity," *American Psychological Association,* January 2009, http://www.apa.org/gradpsych/2009/01/creativity.aspx.

12: Tortured Artist

1. "Depression," *World Health Organization,* February 2017, http://www.who.int/mediacentre/factsheets/fs369/en/.

2. Mark A. Davis, "Understanding the relationship between mood and creativity: A meta-analysis," in *Organizational Behavior and Human Decision Processes* 108, no. 1 (January 2009): 25-38.

3. Psalm 34:17.

13: Stress

Epigraph: John MacArthur, *Drawing Near* (Wheaton, IL: Crossway, 1993). See the entry for October 16.

1. Isaiah 26:3.

14: People Pleasing

1. Matt Chandler, Eric Geiger, and Josh Patterson, *Creature of the Word* (Nashville, TN: B&H, 2012), 28.

16: Perfectionism

Epigraph: Brené Brown, *The Gifts of Imperfection* (Center City, MN: Hazelden, 2010), 56.

17: Performance Mentality

Epigraph: David Platt, *What Did Jesus Really Mean When He Said Follow Me?* (Chicago, IL: Tyndale, 2013), 13.

1. Ephesians 2:8-9 NLT.
2. Matthew 11:28 NLT.

19: Unleash Creativity Introduction

1. Joshua 5:6.
2. Andrew Tate, "Benefits of Walking: Why The Greatest Minds Take Long Walks," *Canva,* February 7, 2016, https://designschool .canva.com/blog/taking-long-walks/.
3. May Wong, "Stanford Study Finds Walking Improves Creativity," *Stanford News,* April 24, 2014, https://news.stanford .edu/2014/04/24/walking-vs-sitting-042414/.

20: Cultivate Your Creativity

1. "Lucille Ball," *Biography,* https://www.biography.com/people/lucille-ball-9196958.

21: Release Your Uniqueness

1. Neil Herndon, "The Odds Are Against You: Things More Likely Than Winning The Powerball," *Forbes,* January 13, 2016, https://www.forbes.com/sites/archenemy/2016/01/13/the-odds-are-against-you-things-more-likely-than-winning-the-powerball/#18dba4644687.
2. Tanya Basu, "Feeling Lucky? How Lotto Odds Compare to Shark Attacks and Lightning Strikes," *National Geographic,* December 21, 2013, https://news.nationalgeographic.com/news/2013/12/131219-lottery-odds-winning-mega-million-lotto.
3. Mel Robbins, "How to Stop Screwing Yourself Over," *TEDx,* June 11, 2011, https://youtu.be/Lp7E973zozc.
4. Luke 12:7; Psalm 139:13.
5. Shefali Sahasrabudhe, "Why Are Fingerprints Unique?" *Science ABC,* 2015, https://www.scienceabc.com/innovation/why-are-fingerprints-unique-and-why-do-we-have-them.html.
6. Brené Brown, *Rising Strong* (New York, NY: Random House, 2017), 195.
7. Ephesians 2:10 NLT.

22: Engage in Community

1. Paul Tripp, *Whiter Than Snow* (Wheaton, IL: Crossway, 2008), 147.

23: Allow Yourself to Dream

1. Alison Doyle, "Top 15 Dream Jobs for Kids," *The Balance,* Updated July 6, 2017, https://www.thebalance.com/top-kids-dream-jobs-2062280.
2. Numbers 22:21-41.

24: Tolerate Failure

1. Rachel Gillett, "21 Highly Successful People Who Rebounded After Getting Fired," *Business Insider,* October 6, 2015, http://www .businessinsider.com/successful-people-who-were-fired-2015-10.
2. 1 Peter 5:6.

25: Identity in Christ

Epigraph: Cited in Myriah Towner, "'Put God First in Everything You Do': Denzel Washington Delivers Inspirational Commencement

Address Encouraging College Grads to Fail Big and Take Chances," *Dailymail.com,* May 11, 2015, http://www.dailymail.co.uk/news/article-3077161/.

1. Colossians 2:7 NLT.

26: Vulnerability

1. Romans 8:28.

27: Invite Holy Spirit

Epigraph: Charles Spurgeon, "A Revival Promise" (sermon delivered on January 11, 1874), *Christian Classics Ethereal Library,* https://www.ccel.org/ccel/spurgeon/sermons20.ii.html.

1. Romans 8:9-11.

2. Galatians 5:22.

3. 1 Corinthians 2:4-5 NLT.

4. Robert Briner, *Roaring Lambs: A Gentle Plan to Radically Change Your World* (Grand Rapids, MI: Zondervan, 1993), 141.

5. Cited in Carlos Rodriguez, "The Faith Comeback of Mel Gibson," *Happy Sonship,* October 21 2016, http://www.happysonship.com/mel-gibson/.

28: Total Surrender

1. Mark 14:35-36 MSG.

2. Joe La Puma, "The Deep End," *Complex,* Oct./Nov. 2015, http://www.complex.com/music/justin-bieber-interview-2015-cover-story.

3. Faye James, "'Mark my words Jesus loves you': Hillsong devotee Justin Bieber kicks off his Sydney show by scrawling a Christian message on stage," *Dailymail.com,* March 15 2017, http://www.dailymail.co.uk/tvshowbiz/article-4318536/.

4. *Strong's Exhaustive Concordance of the Bible,* s.v. 5456 sagad; *New American Standard Exhaustive Concordance of the Bible,* 5th ed. (La Habra, CA: Foundation Publications, 1998), s.v. worship.

5. Oswald Chambers, *My Utmost for His Highest* (Grand Rapids, MI: Discovery House, 1935). See the entry for August 4.

29: You Are Chosen

1. Exodus 26:7.

2. Ephesians 1:4-6 NLT.

3. John Piper, "Ten Reasons to Revel in Being Chosen," *Desiring God,* October 27, 2015, https://www.desiringgod.org/articles/ten-reasons-to-revel-in-being-chosen.

31: That's a Wrap

1. "C.S. Lewis," *Biography.com,* October 31, 2017, https://www.biography.com/people/cs-lewis-9380969.

Closing Credits

God, the pages of this book cannot contain all You've done in my life. I'm forever grateful.

A thank-you seems so tiny in comparison to all my husband, Matt, does to serve, lead, and love our family so well. I love you and the way you pursue adventure and think outside the box, and I adore how you invented our family freestyle rap. And to Maddox and Zoey, the dance-crazed littles who inspire us to embrace childlike wonder daily—you are gifts from God.

Mom and Dad, you've spoken life into me since the beginning. Thank you for never killing my creativity and for teaching me to dream. To my siblings who always starred in my "productions" growing up, may we always color outside the lines together.

Jeremy, Erin, Ariana, Michelle, Anna, Jessie, Elisha, Mindy, Pete, and Danielle—thank you for your wisdom investment in this project.

Michelle, Brayden, Melinda, and Melody, you're the original creative crew that gave this book the legs to stand. Thank you, thank you, thank you.

To the professionals who make working fun—Dan, your high-five the day you saw this project ninja-chopped the doubt I had surrounding this calling. Barb, because you believed in this message, it will go farther than I had ever dared to dream. Gene, thank you for your kindness. You're the ultimate word wizard who communicates in such a powerful way. Janelle, thank you for designing the inside pages of this book with such loving care. And to Connie and to the rest of the Harvest House crew, I've cried happy tears at the thought of you. Thank you for forcing me to learn how to spell "courageous" and for pursuing divine inspiration along the way.

Kara, Cindy, Hayley, Cara, Maria, Brynn, and my Redeemer church family—from the frantic texts to the prayer requests, I am so thankful for you lifting up this project and the people who worked on it. Your prayers, discernment, friendship, support, and wisdom in my life are invaluable.

And to you, dear creative, shine on.

Image Credits

The icons in this book are © by Keep Calm and Vector, AVIcon, Introwiz1, DStarky, StockVector, marinastash, AF studio/Shutterstock.

Background art is © by Lera Efremova, Ozz Design, Yourbookkeeper, Pranch/Shutterstock.

Coloring illustrations on pages 35, 65, 99, and 113 are © by Danielle Rogers.

Additional coloring pages are © by ImHope, Maria Butenko/Shutterstock.

Animal drawing on page 38 is by Matt Randle.